Teach Yourself
Machine Embroidery

OTHER BOOKS AVAILABLE FROM CHILTON
Robbie Fanning, Series Editor

Contemporary Quilting

All Quilt Blocks Are Not Square, by Debra Wagner

Barbara Johannah's Crystal Piecing

The Complete Book of Machine Quilting, Second Edition, by Robbie and Tony Fanning

Contemporary Quilting Techniques, by Pat Cairns

Creative Triangles for Quilters, by Janet B. Elwin

Dye It! Paint It! Quilt It!, by Joyce Mori and Cynthia Myerberg

Fast Patch, by Anita Hallock

Precision Pieced Quilts Using the Foundation Method, by Jane Hall and Dixie Haywood

The Quilter's Guide to Rotary Cutting, by Donna Poster

Scrap Quilts Using Fast Patch, by Anita Hallock

Stars Galore and Even More, by Donna Poster

Stitch 'n' Quilt, by Kathleen Eaton

Super Simple Quilts, by Kathleen Eaton

Three-Dimensional Pieced Quilts, by Jodie Davis

Craft Kaleidoscope

The Banner Book, Ruth Ann Lowery

The Crafter's Guide to Glues, by Tammy Young

Creating and Crafting Dolls, by Eloise Piper and Mary Dilligan

Fabric Crafts and Other Fun with Kids, by Susan Parker Beck and Charlou Lunsford

Quick and Easy Ways with Ribbon, by Ceci Johnson

Learn Bearmaking, by Judi Maddigan

Stamping Made Easy, by Nancy Ward

Creative Machine Arts

ABCs of Serging, by Tammy Young and Lori Bottom

Affordable Heirlooms, by Edna Powers and Gaye Kriegel

Alphabet Stitchery by Hand & Machine, by Carolyn Vosburg Hall

The Button Lover's Book, by Marilyn Green

Claire Shaeffer's Fabric Sewing Guide

The Complete Book of Machine Embroidery, by Robbie and Tony Fanning

Craft an Elegant Wedding, by Tammy Young and Naomi Baker

Distinctive Serger Gifts and Crafts, by Naomi Baker and Tammy Young

Gail Brown's All-New Instant Interiors

Hold It! How to Sew Bags, Totes, Duffels, Pouches, and More, by Nancy Restuccia

How to Make Soft Jewelry, by Jackie Dodson

Innovative Serging, by Gail Brown and Tammy Young

The New Creative Serging Illustrated, by Pati Palmer, Gail Brown, and Sue Green

Quick Napkin Creations, by Gail Brown

Second Stitches: Recycle as You Sew, by Susan Parker

Serge a Simple Project, by Tammy Young and Naomi Baker

Serge Something Super for Your Kids, by Cindy Cummins

Sew Any Patch Pocket, by Claire Shaeffer

Sew Any Set-In Pocket, by Claire Shaeffer

Sew Sensational Gifts, by Naomi Baker and Tammy Young

Sewing and Collecting Vintage Fashions, by Eileen MacIntosh

Shirley Botsford's Daddy's Ties

Soft Gardens: Make Flowers with Your Sewing Machine, by Yvonne Perez-Collins

The Stretch & Sew Guide to Sewing Knits, by Ann Person

Twenty Easy Machine-Made Rugs, by Jackie Dodson

The Ultimate Serger Answer Guide, by Naomi Baker, Gail Brown and Cindy Kacynski

Know Your Serger Series,
by Tammy Young and Naomi Baker

Know Your baby lock

Sew & Serge Series,
by Jackie Dodson and Jan Saunders

Sew & Serge Pillows! Pillows! Pillows!

Sew & Serge Terrific Textures

StarWear

Dazzle, by Linda Fry Kenzle

Embellishments, by Linda Fry Kenzle

Jan Saunders' Wardrobe Quick-Fixes

Make It Your Own, by Lori Bottom and Ronda Chaney

Mary Mulari's Garments with Style

A New Serge in Wearable Art, by Ann Boyce

Pattern-Free Fashions, by Mary Lee Trees Cole

Shirley Adams' Belt Bazaar

Sweatshirts with Style, by Mary Mulari

Teach Yourself to Sew Better,
by Jan Saunders

A Step-by-Step Guide to Your New Home

A Step-by-Step Guide to Your Sewing Machine

Teach Yourself
Machine Embroidery

Easy Decorative Stitching Using Any Sewing Machine

SUSAN ROCK

Chilton
BOOK COMPANY
Radnor, Pennsylvania

Published in Radnor, Pennsylvania 19089, by Chilton Book Company

Cover design Anthony Jacobson
Interior design Stan Green/Green Graphics
Color photography by Donna Chiarelli
Black-and-white photography by William H. Jacob of Perspective Studios
Line drawings by Monica Cote and Marc Gagne

Manufactured in the United States of America

Cataloging-in-Publication Data
Rock, Susan.
   Teach yourself machine embroidery : easy decorative stitching using any sewing machine / Susan Rock.
      p.   cm.
   Includes bibliographical references and index.
   ISBN 0-8019-8522-6
   1. Embroidery, Machine. I. Title.
TT772.R63   1996   96-17853
746.44'028—dc20   CIP

1 2 3 4 5 6 7 8 9 0   5 4 3 2 1 0 9 8 7 6

Acknowledgments

Thanks to all of you this book is born!

Thanks to my husband for his never-ending encouragement and for utilizing his vast computer knowledge to help someone who really didn't want to know how the computer worked but loved the end result.

Thanks also go to my students. Over the past few years many of my students have asked whether or not I had written "that" book yet. I always had a litany of excuses until one day Jen said, "It doesn't have to be an exhaustive study of everything you'll ever know." And then over her shoulder as she was parting she said, "It's better to write something now than everything never." And so here in *Teach Yourself Machine Embroidery* are the spruced up versions of all those vast piles of notes on scraps of paper filed under "ideas" in my file cabinet. I share them with you that they may not have been written in vain.

I offer a sincere thank you to the following companies for the loan of sewing machines and sergers: Viking Husqvarna; Pfaff American Sales Corp.; Singer Sewing Co.; New Home Sewing Machine Company; and Bernina of America, Inc. Thanks to Passap-USA for its fine iron; to Mundial for dress maker and embroidery scissors; to Decart, Inc., Deco Art, and Delta for fabric paint. Thanks also to Ghee's, HeatnBond, Waverly Fabric, Schmetz Needle Corporation, Madeira USA, and Madeira Mkt. for generous supplies for use in the many projects in this book.

A special thanks to my friend and fellow embroider Peg Laflam for camaraderie and the loan of her marbled fabric/couched thread vest. Without the support and expertise of the fine people at Chilton Book Company, including Susan Keller, Christine Sweeney, and Robbie Fanning, the line-drawing artists Monica Cote and Marc Gagne, and black-and-white photographer Bill Jacob this book simply would have been a record of one person's sewing journey instead of a step-by-step guide to the pleasures of machine embroidery.

Contents

Foreword

People who love machine embroidery have an active grapevine. We exchange ideas and enthusiasms in person at guilds, seminars, and classes, and exchange them long-distance by postcard, letter, phone, newsletter, magazine, and now on-line. When Susan Rock's article on making machine-embroidered yardage appeared in *Threads Magazine* (April/May 1991), the grapevine buzzed: "Did you see? . . . gorgeous! . . . innovative! . . . we want more!"

At last, we have more—this fascinating book. The grapevine will activate again. I predict excited discussions:

- about her thorough knowledge of threads ("Did you see the part about thread nap—how if you wind thread onto a bobbin and use it for a top thread, you're stitching against the nap and the thread may break or snarl? You should wind it onto a second bobbin so the nap runs the correct way.")

- about her whimsical uses of single motifs of colorful thread on top of patterned fabric (thread hearts on top of printed hearts, satin-stitch blobs on top of printed rectangles, and more)

- about her ideas for using built-in decorative stitches (making beautiful four-sided motifs, even with stitches as simple as the blindhem).

But you don't have to be experienced in machine embroidery to enjoy this book. Susan provides detailed information for every level of student, as well as step-by-step instructions for many creative projects. With this book, you will easily teach yourself machine embroidery. Then come join our grapevine.

ROBBIE FANNING
Founding Series Editor and co-author,
The Complete Book of Machine Embroidery

Part One

Getting Started

Introduction

Embroidery is a type of ornamental needlework used to create intricate designs on fabric—the clothes we wear, the decorative pillows and table scarves that grace our homes, even objects we use every day, like eyeglass holders and wallets. Originally worked by hand, embroidery became mechanized in the eighteenth century, almost one hundred years before Elias Howe invented a two-thread lock stitch sewing machine.

Although machines existed to produce embroidery, it wasn't until the 1890s, when many people began to explore the artistic uses of the home sewing machine, that sewing machine embroidery became a possibility. At the turn of the century, the Singer Sewing Machine Company proved that nearly all hand embroidery could be duplicated on a straight stitch machine! In their book *Singer Instructions for Art Embroidery and Lace Work*, first published in 1922, Singer employees demonstrated almost every hand embroidery technique on sewing machines in the Singer work room.

Since then home sewers and embroiderers have come into their own with swing needle (also known as zigzag) machines, pre-programmed patterns, and computer assisted machines. These machines give us endless creative opportunities. We may simply stitch the programmed design or change the design by manipulating the stitch width and length. We may use our zigzag stitch alone or in combination. We may be inspired to develop our own pattern designs on a computer assisted machine.

Machine embroidery is fun, absorbing, and relaxing. A perfect hobby for our busy lives, machine embroidery is three times faster than embroidering by hand. Sewing machines create precise stitches that can be repeated again and again to quickly embellish clothing, household items, gifts, and crafts.

I had been a hand embroiderer for many years, but always felt a bit restricted by all the rules, especially in canvas work, where there is only one correct place to insert the needle. Surface stitchery is somewhat freer, giving me choices about where to put the next stitch, but when I found machine embroidery—or rather when it found me—I felt like I had been set free.

Some people may say, "Yes . . . but I'm no good with machines. They always act up." Well, I have a solution to that problem. First, get to know your sewing machine. Whether it is an old friend or a shiny new one, reread your owner's manual. Experiment with the buttons and dials. If you still have questions, visit your dealer. Most dealers know their machines inside and out and have attended in-depth classes. It also helps to stitch a sampler of each of the patterns your machine sews. Often people who admire machine embroidery and try it find that although they have not excelled at other arts or crafts, machine embroidery is where they shine.

Is it art or is it craft? In the ten years that I sat on the stitchery jury of the League of New Hampshire, we often bandied about this very subject. We decided that whether we called it art or craft, embroidery of superior workmanship, of lasting quality, and integrity was the goal. Your work will easily reach these criteria by following the course of study in *Teach Yourself Machine Embroidery*, which contains over fifty wonderful projects ready for you to stitch. The design work and planning are done; just the fun of embroidering is left for you. Be creative, but most of all have fun. I often tell my students you can't make a mistake in machine embroidery! Stitch over it if it does not please you, or cut it up and use it for another embroidery project. Once you try machine embroidery, you will spend many pleasant hours creating beautiful objects for yourself and your loved ones.

From Bobbins to Zigzag

Understanding Your Sewing Machine

A tool is but the extension of a man's hand.
—Henry Ward Beecher

Machine embroidery is a lot more fun when you have the right sewing machine and know how to use its features and functions. As the folks at Singer demonstrated so many years ago, you don't need a fancy sewing machine to make machine embroidery. Indeed, in Chapter Five we explore the versatility of the straight stitch. But the complicated stitches, sophisticated accessories, and computer memory offered by today's sewing machines give us thousands of options not available on the basic straight stitch/zigzag machine. If you are in need of a new sewing machine, read this chapter, then shop around and listen to several sales presentations. Make sure you bring with you the Shopper's Checklist for a Sewing Machine in the reference section at the back of this book. It will help you organize your research. Today's sewing machines, with their sophisticated features, can cost more than a refrigerator or a washing machine, and so it pays to know as much about them as you can before you buy.

But if you already own a sewing machine without the full array of fancy gadgets, don't panic. You can still do machine embroidery. Instead of using the first part of this chapter as a buying guide, use it to review the features and

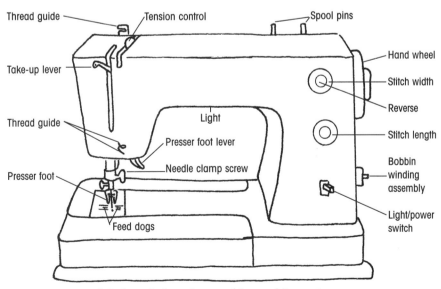

1.1 A typical sewing machine and its parts.

functions available on your machine. Some are absolutely necessary while others add to the ease and enjoyment of this exciting art. Use the second part of this chapter to review the operation and maintenance of your machine.

Whether you plan to buy a new sewing machine or are happily utilizing a machine you already own, this chapter can show you how specific sewing machine options come into play during the machine embroidery process.

USEFUL SEWING MACHINE OPTIONS

FEED DOGS AND PRESSER FEET

Feed dogs and presser feet make consistent stitches possible. Feed dogs move the fabric along—making it ready to form a new stitch.

Presser feet hold the fabric tightly and smoothly against the feed dogs while stitches are formed. Choose presser feet by evaluating both the type of stitch and the fabric to be sewn. A straight stitch demands a flat-bottomed presser foot that maintains good contact with the fabric and the feed dogs. When sewing on fine or very heavy fabric it is especially important that the presser foot and feed dog work together to move the fabric along.

Feed Dogs

Feed dogs are the teethlike metal pieces under the presser foot that rise up to meet the fabric each time the needle penetrates the fabric and a new stitch is formed. As they rise, they move the fabric one stitch length forward, making possible even, consistently open or dense stitches (Fig. 1.2). The distance they move the fabric is determined by the stitch length and the thickness or thinness of the fabric being sewn. All sewing machines are calibrated using medium weight fabric. This means that when sewing on a medium weight fabric, the sewing machine will always sew, for example, 2.5mm between each stitch. When sewn on a light weight or very heavy

Even stitching

Gaps in stitching

Piled-up stitching

1.2 Feed dogs must be used properly to ensure consistent stitches.

fabric, this same length of 2.5mm will produce a constant stitch length, but it may not be the same size as when sewing on the medium weight fabric. The stitch length will probably be longer on fine fabrics and shorter on heavy weight fabrics. This difference can cause puckering because the sewing machine may not advance enough thread for the required stitch. If that happens to you, try decreasing the stitch length on fine fabrics and increasing it on heavy fabrics. If there is still puckering, decrease both the needle and the bobbin tension a small amount, making sure that both tensions still produce a balanced stitch. Check to make sure that the bottom of the presser foot is smooth.

In order for the machine to do its job effectively the sewer need only guide the fabric as it goes under the presser foot. When the fabric is pushed the stitches will have gaps. Conversely, stitches pile up when the fabric is held back.

The ability to lower the feed dogs is important in free motion embroidery. The lowered feed dogs allow the embroiderer to move the fabric in any direction and to determine the length and width of each stitch. (More about free motion embroidery in Chapters Five and Six.)

Many machines have a knob which causes the feed dogs to be lowered beneath the flat bed of the sewing machine. This is ideal. You may find this feature listed under darning in the owner's manual.

Some manufacturers provide a small plastic or metal plate that simply covers the feed dogs. The principle disadvantage to this cover is that it decreases the amount of space between the bed of the sewing machine and the end of the needle at its highest position, making it difficult, if not impossible, for the embroidery hoop to fit under the needle. It becomes necessary, therefore, to remove the needle every time the hoop is to be placed under the needle. The second disadvantage is that the raised feed dog cover creates a hump under the hooped fabric, preventing it from laying flat on the bed. This often causes skipped stitches and makes it more difficult to control the hoop.

If your current sewing machine has a plastic cover plate you can still do machine embroidery by keeping these potential problems in mind and taking precautions. If you are contemplating the purchase of a new sewing machine look for a machine in which the feed dogs drop easily.

Dual Feed Dogs

An attachment called a walking foot, which acts as a second feed dog on the top of the fabric, is available from most manufacturers. Generic models can be purchased from your dealer or through a mail order catalog.

Pfaff sewing machines and most industrial machines have a dual feed dog mechanism built into the machine. Along with the regular feed dog built into the bed of the sewing machine, there is a second feed dog that can be lowered into operation. When in use, it rides on top of the fabric and becomes part of the presser foot. This feature helps to eliminate the shifting of fabric layers while ensuring that check and plaid fabrics join evenly. In machine embroidery, when the fabric is often highly embellished or textured, the dual feed moves both the bottom and the top fabric along simultaneously. Dual feed is helpful in machine embroidery when stitching dense pre-programmed stitches so that no thread build up or gaps in the pattern occur.

Transparent Presser Feet

You will find it easier to line up patterns and to see exactly where the next stitch will be when you can see through the presser foot. A transparent presser foot often has marked lines on it which help to guide the fabric, thus insuring a straight row of stitching.

Presser Foot Lever

Presser foot levers are located on the side or back of the machine; either placement works effectively.

The Viking, Pfaff, and Singer sewing machines have a feature that raises the lever to a higher position than normal to facilitate the placement of heavy fabric or a machine embroidery hoop on the bed of the sewing machine. Many times this feature has helped me avoid marring fabric and made it possible for me to place an extra wide embroidery hoop under the foot without removing the foot itself.

The Bernina and New Home machines have presser foot knee lifters of metal and rubber that are inserted into sockets on the lower right side of the machines. The lever is operated with the right knee, which simultaneously raises or lowers the presser foot and feed dogs. Both hands are then free to guide the fabric. I find this very useful in machine embroidery.

Sewing Machine Feet and Other Accessories

Some machines on the market have under a dozen feet while others have thirty to fifty! Most new machines have snap on feet that are easy to exchange. The Bernina, for example, has a clamp lever that is easily raised and lowered to change its large number of feet.

There are a handful of feet and accessories common to most machines that I find helpful in machine embroidery.

- *Satin stitch foot or embroidery foot:* This foot has a slight hollow on the underside. The hollow area allows the foot to glide over thick embroidery.

- *Darning foot or embroidery foot:* This foot, used for free motion embroidery and darning, is usually round and open in the center. Its purpose is to improve visibility and to insure that there is pressure on the fabric against the bed of the sewing machine at the moment a stitch is formed. This prevents the fabric from following the needle to the up position and causing wear to the thread. The easiest embroidery feet to use are constructed of clear plastic. Some metal darning feet have part of the front cut away for better visibility. If your metal darning foot does not have a cut-away, ask your dealer to use a metal file and cut off one third of the round portion of the foot.

- *Feed dog cover:* It is a good idea to cover the feed dogs if lowering them is not an option. If a feed dog cover is not available you can still cover the feed dogs with tape. Be sure to set the stitch length at zero. That way there will be less friction on the tape because the feed dogs will barely move. Make a hole in the tape so that the needle can enter the bobbin case.

- *Pintucking or cording foot:* This foot has a more pronounced rounded groove than the satin stitch or embroidery foot. It may, in fact, have as many as nine grooves. It allows you to stitch over or beside cording, tucks, and gimp.

- *Quilting bar or edge guide:* Use either accessory as a guide for straight seams when the stitching line is wider than the graduated measuring guide lines on the throat plate of the sewing machine. Quilting bars and edge guides are also useful when the bed of the sewing machine is covered with the fabric being stitched, thus obscuring the stitch guides. When you use a quilting bar, keep your eye on the bar as it glides along the previous row of stitching.

- *Fringe foot or marker foot or tailor tacking foot:* This foot creates loops along the stitching line. It can be used to mark a pattern or as a decorative stitch.

- *Open toe embroidery foot:* Of construction similar to that of the satin stitch foot, the open toe embroidery foot sports one significant difference—the front center is cut away to improve visibility.

NEEDLE AND THREAD MECHANISMS

In our grandmothers' sewing machines, the needle simply went up and down. Today's machines offer options that allow one to move the needle left, right, or center as well as stop in either the up or the down position. Read on to see how these features and others will assist you.

Needle Stop (Up or Down)

The needle may stop in the highest or lowest position. This is a big advantage in machine embroidery because when the needle is in the down position, in either the regular or the free motion embroidery mode, you may stop the machine, move or turn the fabric, and begin stitching where you left off. The needle up position is useful when applying beads by machine and for regular end-row stitching. When you are embroidering with the presser foot attached, the needle up position allows you to complete a row of stitching without manipulating the hand wheel to release the needle from the fabric.

Both the Bernina and the Viking can regulate the needle stop position with the foot control. Tap the foot control to change the needle to the opposite position.

Walking foot

Darning foot

Quilting bar

Embroidery foot

Fringe foot

Feed dog cover

Cording foot

1.3 Useful sewing machine feet.

Horizontal Needle Position

Certain techniques are easier when your machine can change its needle position to the right or to the left of its center position. When you want to sew on the edge of a fabric and do not want to raise the presser foot and move the fabric, you can move your needle instead. In addition, this feature can be used to create unusual designs. An interesting pattern of stitches can be formed by changing the needle position to the right or the left. Several machines on the market today have this feature; one of the widest ranges offered is nineteen needle positions.

Twin or Triple Needles and Guarded Width

Another welcome feature is the capacity to use a twin or triple needle. These needles are manufactured on a single shaft with the needles side by side. The result is parallel rows of straight, zigzag, and some programmed stitches. Twin needles can only be used with a zigzag machine.

When the guarded width is selected the machine will only swing the needle as wide as the hole in the presser foot and throat plate, decreasing the possibility of broken needles.

Slant Needles

Unlike most needles, a slant needle is not perpendicular to the bed of the machine. Usually the needle slants slightly toward the sewer. It is usually easy to see the slant by looking at the needle from the left side of the sewing machine. If you are unsure of the needle angle in relation to the sewing machine, ask your dealer.

Beware of slant needle machines. Many of the older models allow the hoop to move freely in the direction of the slant but are crabby when moving away from the slant of the needle. This creates an embroidery that is not smooth.

Changing Needles and Presser Feet

Examine the ease with which a needle is changed. Do you need a screw driver to remove the needle? Ideally there will be a little knob that turns easily by hand, making it fast and easy to switch needles during embroidery.

You may find this feature useful, for example, when embroidering a piece that has both dense stitching and beadwork. You will need a large needle to embroider the stitches and a small needle to apply the beads. Remember, when applying beads by machine, the blade of the needle must be small enough to pass through the center of the bead, thus necessitating a change of needles mid-embroidery.

How easily are the presser foot and ankle changed? Can you remove the presser foot and ankle by twisting a knob? Do they snap on or do you need a screw driver?

Horizontal Spool Holder or Pin

The option of a horizontal spool holder is a real plus. It allows the thread to reel off the spool from right to left, thus decreasing upper thread breakage because there is less tugging on the thread as it leaves the spool. With a vertical spool pin the spool of thread rotates as the thread leaves the spool, thereby tugging the thread, which may result in breakage of some metallic threads.

When the thread leaves the spool freely the machine can make nice smooth embroidery stitches. The Viking 1200 has an adjustable spool pin holder that can be used in a vertical or horizontal position. Many notions catalogs and sewing departments carry a horizontal spool holder that attaches to the spool pin of your sewing machine.

Dual Spool Holder

Does the machine have two spool pins (Fig. 1.4)? The second spool pin means you can stitch with two colors of thread through the needle or accommodate twin needle sewing. Dual spool holders eliminate the need to use a coffee cup placed at the back of your sewing machine to hold the second spool. Both spools feed more smoothly as a result. The second spool holder also allows the filling of a bobbin while the sewing machine remains threaded. When threading with two top threads follow the manufacturer's instructions. This will usually include separating the two threads on either side of the tension disk and just before the needle.

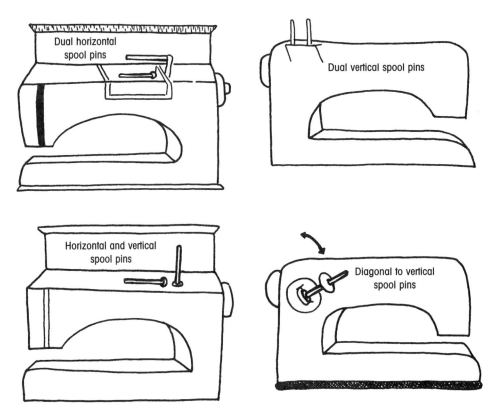

1.4 Four types of spool pins found on sewing machines.

Built-in Needle Threader

If you really want to pamper yourself, go for the gold—a built-in needle threader! It's a real frustration saver if your eyes aren't all they used to be. Even if you can see as well as the day you were born it's still to be coveted because decorative machine embroidery threads, particularly the metallic threads, tend to split their blunt ends when pointed toward the eye of the needle.

Thread Cutter

All current model machines have a built-in thread cutter usually located on the left rear of the machine near the needle. Older models are often without a cutter, which means you must pick up a pair of scissors to clip the threads every time you finish a row of stitching.

The current model Singer machine has a built-in thread cutter in the presser bar lifter. Babylock's Esante and Brother's PC 7500 can both be programmed to automatically cut the thread after the last stitch.

Needle and Bobbin Tension Adjustment

Often it is necessary to adjust the tensions of both the needle thread and the bobbin thread. Look for an adjustment dial on the left front of the machine. Hopefully, it is numbered. This dial regulates the amount of tension put on the spool thread. Generally the higher the number the tighter the tension. You may learn more about needle and bobbin tension in "Operating Your Sewing Machine" later in this chapter.

There are two kinds of adjustable bobbin tensions. A removable bobbin case adjusts the tension on the outside of the bobbin case, usually with the larger screw. A drop-in bobbin with a built-in bobbin case lies flat in the machine, under the needle plate. Usually the tension screw is to the right front and has a number scale beside it. Check your sewing machine manual.

BOBBINS

One can never have too many bobbins. Careful filling (not running the sewing machine too fast) and a storage box just for bobbins provide frustration free embroidery.

Bobbin Case Accessibility

Is the bobbin case easy to reach? To test, attach the sewing table, and then try to remove the bobbin case. Did you have to stand on your head or remove the sewing table? The best situation is when the sewing table flips open or the accessory box swings away to expose the bobbin case.

Bobbin Winder

A bobbin on which the thread is wound firmly and evenly is ideal. Because some machines have better bobbin winding devices than others, you should try filling a couple of bobbins before you select a new machine. Does the machine wind bobbins without difficulty or does it wind them unevenly? Uneven winding can be fixed easily by most dealers. Notice if the thread has a tendency to fall out of the thread guides as the bobbin is filling. When this happens the thread is usually wound evenly but loosely across the bobbin. Poor quality stitches are the end result, so make sure the thread is properly situated in the bobbin winding thread guides, rethreading the machine if necessary.

Bobbin Thread Monitor

Most current model machines have a wonderful feature that alerts the user when the bobbin thread is about to run out. A light or screen will begin flashing when the bobbin is down to its last three to five yards. The amount depends on the weight of the thread. The correct bobbin for the machine model must be used for this feature to work. It usually requires a plastic bobbin.

Bobbin Hole Size

It is handy if the bobbin used in the bobbin case also fits on the spool pin holder. This will permit the use of more than one thread at a time on a single spool pin holder machine.

It is also useful if the bobbin has wound poorly. When this happens, place the poorly

filled bobbin on the spool pin and an empty bobbin on the bobbin winder and rewind the bobbin.

THROAT PLATES

There are straight stitch and zigzag throat plates. When sewing and embroidering, it is important to use the correct throat plate. The throat plate on a zigzag machine has a larger opening to accommodate the swing of the needle; this larger opening may cause the fabric to waver up and down with the movement of the needle (Fig. 1.5). If you are straight stitching while using a zigzag throat plate, the fabric will not be held flat on the throat plate and a poor quality stitch will be formed. If this happens, ask your dealer for a straight stitch throat plate (Fig. 1.6).

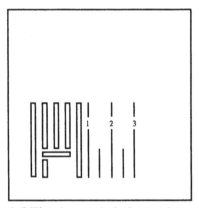

1.5 The zigzag stitch throat plate.

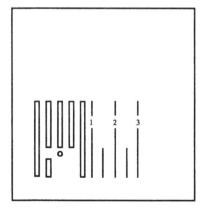

1.6 The straight stitch throat plate.

STITCHING FEATURES

Embroidering with a straight stitch machine is creative in and of itself, but your creative options increase with each stitching feature your machine offers.

Zigzag or Swing Needle

Although one can do elegant embroidery on a straight stitch machine, a machine that zigzags augments your embroidery capabilities one hundred percent. The width of the zigzag (or swing needle) should range from just the slightest movement right to left to a width of at least 6mm. Some of the newer machines have a 9mm wide stitch. This wide swing of the needle allows immense opportunity for the build up of thread, forming texture and pattern and making possible the blending of color in your embroidery.

Some machines only allow the increase of the zigzag width in increments of 0.5mm. This will be confining on occasion, such as when wanting to gradually increase or decrease the width of the zigzag at a corner. A knob for adjustment of width and length gives a smoother graduation.

1.7 Today's zigzag sewing machines allow the sewer to elongate a stitch while maintaining even thread density.

Satin Stitch Extension

Most zigzag sewing machines allow pre-programmed stitches to be stretched in length. Current models go a step further and ensure that the elongated pattern has the same thread density as the original size (Fig. 1.7). This is an important feature when machine embroidering.

Start/Stop Button

This button, usually located on the front of the machine near the needle, replaces the foot control. To use this feature on the Singer, the Brother, and the New Home sewing machines, unplug the foot control at the machine. When activated, the sewing machine will first sew a few stitches slowly and then run at the speed selected by the speed setting lever. This is useful in machine embroidery when sewing long rows of pre-programmed stitches and when stitching the large maxi programs.

Speed Setting

Most current models allow the seamstress to choose the speed of the machine. The speed of the motor can be decreased to one third or one half the regular speed by using a cursor, lever, command ball, or button. This causes the machine to sew at the selected speed even when the foot control is fully depressed. This feature helps give added control when embroidering intricate patterns by allowing consistent speed, which helps decrease jerking or a sudden serge of speed, both of which may break the needle or thread or cause puckers.

Single Stitch

The ability to start and stop after a single stitch is also of great value to the embroiderer. You may want to take a stitch, for example, and then apply a bead and take another stitch. Or take a stitch and then stop and pull the bobbin thread to the surface. This will only be possible if your machine takes one stitch at a time or you use the hand wheel to take a single stitch.

The single stitch feature will help you if you are doing an embellishment in which a long stitch is required. This feature can be used to stitch a pre-programmed pattern. It is used to advantage in "Patterns in Fours," a project found in Chapter Seven.

Stitching a single pattern is useful when several patterns have been placed in memory and only one series is needed, such as with a monogram.

Pattern Start

When this function is activated the machine automatically returns to the beginning of the pattern selected. This is useful in embroidery when you want to start consecutive rows of stitching at the same place in the pattern. This feature also is invaluable for restarting a pattern mid-row. Refer to the "Festive Table Frock" project in Chapter Seven for more detail about restarting a pattern mid-row.

Most sewing machines and manuals show a pattern syllabus. The pattern begins as it is pictured in the syllabus.

Half Pattern

When the half pattern function is activated the machine stops after stitching half of the pattern. This program is used in embroidery to combine patterns or when embroidering corners with a pattern.

Mirror Image Pattern Stitching

In mirror image pattern stitching, the image of the stitch is altered so that the patterns face each other (Fig. 1.8). In reverse-image pattern stitching, the pattern is altered so that motifs face in opposite directions. The Bernina 1630, Pfaff 7550, and Viking #1+ have another mirror imaging feature called vertical and end-to-end mirror imaging respectively. If, for example, a turtle is posed going up, the vertical mirror image makes the next

1.8 Three examples of mirror image pattern stitching.

turtle head downward. The use of mirror image is great fun, since the two rows stitched abutting each other create a new design. It is especially interesting when using alphabets. Look for more creative uses of this feature in Chapter Seven.

Reverse Button

The reverse button causes the machine to stitch backward. Check to find the location of the reverse button. It can be found just above the needle and to the right on most current model machines. Is it easy to engage with your hands resting on the bed of the sewing machine?

All machines except the New Home stitch the selected pattern in reverse. The New Home only stitches straight stitch in reverse. When you push the reverse button while sewing anything but the straight stitch, the New Home will sew locking stitches and then automatically stop. The Viking #1+ sews backward permanently by pressing the reverse button twice in quick succession before starting to sew. The Pfaff has a special feature that allows sewing in reverse permanently until the key is pushed again. Both the Viking and the Pfaff features allow the sewer to guide the fabric with both hands.

Tying Off Stitches

The tie-off feature takes several securing stitches at the beginning and end of each row. Because the Bernina ties on and off stitches that are in memory only, you will need to use the reverse button as a tie-off button. Most other machines will secure stitches at the beginning by sewing a few straight stitches in place. To tie-off at the end, the tie-off button must be pushed again.

FOOT PEDALS, HAND WHEELS, AND OTHER NECESSITIES

The following sewing machine features make life a lot easier and are good things to have when sewing and embroidering by machine.

Electronic Foot Pedal

An electronic foot pedal allows the machine to stop instantly when you move your foot away. This prevents you from stitching beyond where you wish to stitch. It also returns the needle to the highest or lowest position automatically. Additionally, it enables the sewer to take one stitch at a time, or to increase the speed slowly rather than in a burst, which may be uncontrollable.

Most new models have a retractable cord built into the foot pedal, which is very handy when traveling with your machine. The Bernina machines also have a retractable machine cord. On all other machines, this cord must be coiled up by hand when it is removed from the outlet.

Hand Wheel

Be sure to manipulate the hand wheel when trying out a new machine. Some machine hand wheels are rounded, which is more difficult for the sewer to grasp. Is the hand wheel easy to manipulate? Is it light weight and comfortable when your hand turns it?

Built-in Light

Most machines have a light near the needle that goes on when the machine is plugged in. Some are better than others! The Bernina has a switch that allows you to turn off the light without turning off the machine. I find this helpful when the light adds too much glare, which is often a problem when sewing with metallic thread. It also is nice to be able to turn off the light if I want to stop sewing in the middle of a row.

Extension Table

Portable machines have variously sized flat surfaces called beds, extension tables, or sewing tables on which to place fabric or an embroidery hoop. This work surface ranges in size from 15" x 11" to 9" x 6". Bring an embroidery hoop with you to test how it fits on the work surface. Check to see that the bed of the sewing machine is large enough so that an 8" hoop is well supported and does not wobble around. This will aid in controlling the hoop in free motion embroidery. Be aware, however, that the removable table that accompanies free-arm sewing machines can be cumbersome to remove and reinsert. This table can also make it difficult to reach the bobbin case, thereby necessitating removal of the table each time you need to get to the bobbin area. Be sure to remove and reinsert the sewing table so you will know how much of a bother it is.

Free-Arm

On many machines it is possible to remove part of the sewing table to reveal an arm approxi-mately 9" long and 3" wide. This smaller surface makes it easier to sew in tight places, such as sleeves. Use a free-arm, for example, when machine embroidering a monogram on the cuff of a sleeve.

Sewing Machine Portability

Can you take it to a class, to Aunt Mary's, and on vacation easily? (I told you machine embroidery is addictive!) How heavy is this sewing machine? Can you carry it out of your house, into your car, and into a class and still have energy to sew? Is the carrying case light weight yet protective? Is there a place to store the instruction booklet, accessories, and foot pedal during the transport? If not, it is easy to leave the foot pedal and cord at home. Just ask my students.

OPERATING YOUR SEWING MACHINE

It is not enough simply to know what to look for in a sewing machine. In order to get the most out of your sewing machine, you must know how to use it properly. While the following instructions apply to most sewing machines, you should always read your owner's manual.

THREADING A SEWING MACHINE

Although threading a sewing machine, for example, may seem fairly straightforward, it is easy to do it incorrectly. Weakened or broken threads may be the result.

Needle Thread

All sewing machines are threaded so that the needle thread goes through a series of guides, through a tension disk, and finally through the needle. Each manufacturer has thread guides located in different places, and it is critically important that you follow the directions for threading in your manual.

When a machine is threaded incorrectly, one of several possible outcomes will occur. A snarled mess may appear under the fabric, the needle thread will break, or no stitch will form. Remember, the purpose of the thread guides is to allow the thread to arrive at the needle smooth and untangled. The thread leaves the spool and goes through about three guides before it enters the tension disks, which regulate the amount of tension on the thread. After the thread leaves the tension disks it goes through one more guide just above the needle and then through the needle. The post that houses the needle moves up and down each time a stitch is formed and, along with the tension disks, regulates the flow of thread ready to form the next stitch.

Bobbin Thread

Each machine winds the bobbin differently. Machines with rotary bobbin cases usually need to have the machine motor disengaged so that the needle does not go up and down as the bobbin is filling. Some machines have a separate motor for the bobbin winder, thus eliminating the need to manipulate the hand wheel.

When winding bobbins, thread leaves the spool and goes through a series of guides that are usually different from those of the thread path to the needle. Again, it is important to follow the prescribed thread path for your machine or there will not be proper tension on the thread as it is wound on the bobbin. It will wind poorly as a result.

Each machine differs in the way in which thread is attached to the bobbin. Improperly attached thread will cause the thread to wind poorly. Do not use a bobbin in which the thread has been wound unsuccessfully as this will affect the quality of the stitch. If you do wind a bobbin incorrectly do not despair; simply remove the spool of thread and replace it with the fouled bobbin. Put an empty bobbin on the bobbin winder and rewind the thread to the new bobbin. You have not wasted any thread. Chances are that you will not have a full bobbin of thread when you rewind because it was loosely wound in the first place. If so, do not add more thread to the bobbin since new thread on top of old thread often does not wind smoothly.

Most bobbins are placed in the bobbin case so that the thread leaves the bobbin in a clockwise manner. Some New Homes machines require counter clockwise insertion. Consult your manual.

Each manufacturer designs the size and shape of its bobbin and bobbin case differently and so they are not interchangeable. Some machines have rotary bobbin cases that are removable while others have drop-in bobbins, in which the bobbin is dropped into a horizontal stationary case. No matter what type of bobbin, the bobbin should fit into the bobbin case so that it rotates freely.

Changing the Needle

Again it is important to follow specific instructions in your sewing machine manual. First, turn off the machine and then turn the hand wheel toward you, bringing the needle to its highest position. Unscrew the needle clamp. Remove the needle and replace it with a new needle by pushing the shaft of the needle all the way up into the screw clamp. A turn and a half is usually enough. If the screw is not opened enough the needle will not go all the way up into the clamp and when a stitch is taken the needle will crash into the bobbin case, damaging the needle and possibly causing the timing of the machine to be disrupted. (This means that the needle and thread do not meet at the proper moment.) Skipped stitches may also occur when the needle is incompletely inserted into the clamp.

If the needle clamp screw is not screwed tightly against the needle, the needle may fall out during sewing. So remember that it is important to insert the needle (with the flat side away from you in most machines) all the way up into the needle clamp. Take one complete stitch with the hand wheel to be sure that the needle has been inserted properly. Then turn on your machine—you are ready to sew.

Adjusting Sewing Machine Tensions

There are two areas of thread tension to be considered in all lock stitch sewing machines—the bobbin thread tension and the needle thread tension. Combined, both types of tension determine how much thread is used for each stitch. They also affect the appearance, wearability, and performance of the stitching. Since sewing machine tension also is a common cause of thread breakage and puckered designs, it is important to understand how increasing and decreasing either the needle or the bobbin tension affects the stitch.

Loose needle thread tension pulls the needle thread to the back of the fabric. Loose bobbin tension causes the needle thread tension to pull the bobbin thread to the surface of the fabric, where it is often seen as a loop. Although this would not be a good stitch to hold a garment together, it is useful as a decorative stitch.

Different threads and fabrics require different tension settings. Polyester thread, for example, requires slightly less tension than rayon. Because thread size affects tension, a 30 wt thread requires less tension than a 40 wt thread.

Needle Tension

Most machines have a tension adjustment dial with numbers ranging from zero to ten, or in some cases, up to fourteen.

Zero usually means no needle tension, four to five means normal dress-making tension, and six or higher means a tight needle thread tension. Some machines have no numbers at all and simply indicate a plus or minus sign on either side of the space on the dial that indicates normal tension. This dial, located on the front or top upper left of most machines, regulates the amount of pressure the tension disks exert on the needle thread as it passes through the tension disks.

Bobbin Cases

There are two types of bobbin cases in domestic sewing machines. A rotary bobbin has a removable bobbin case. A drop-in bobbin has a built-in case and only the bobbin itself is removable. Each type of case has a different tension adjustment method. In addition, some sewing machine manufacturers offer an optional second bobbin case that allows heavier thread to pass under the tension band with less manipulation of

Hints

• It is not enough simply to set the tension dial. The needle tension must be engaged as well. This is done by lowering the presser foot lever. It is easy to overlook this important detail when one is embroidering in the free motion embroidery mode without a presser foot.

• Most often only the needle thread is seen on the front of the fabric.

• When embroidering it is common to lower the needle tension by one or two numbers. This forces the needle thread to be pulled to the back side of the fabric and results in a smooth finished stitch on the surface.

• Decreasing the needle tension also assures that no bobbin thread will be seen on the front of the embroidery. If the opposite were done (the needle tension increased by one or two numbers) the bobbin thread would be pulled to the front of the embroidery. This causes both the bobbin thread and the needle thread to be seen on the surface and is sometimes useful as a decorative approach to a design.

the screw. Bernina calls this a black latch bobbin case.

Rotary Bobbin Tension Adjustment

Adjust the thread in a rotary bobbin by first cleaning the bobbin case of lint. Be particularly diligent about removing lint since even a tiny piece may cause poorly formed stitches. Use a soft brush to clean these areas, and never use a sharp pointed object because it may scratch the polished surface and cause thread to fray and break. Insert a filled bobbin into the case so that the thread will come from the bobbin in a clockwise direction (unless the sewing machine manual directs otherwise).

Feed the thread under the tension spring. There are two screws on most bobbin cases. One is a set screw and holds the tension band in place. It is usually the smaller of the two screws and does not need to be adjusted. The larger screw is the tension screw and is the one that may need adjustment. To adjust the tension screw, hold the bobbin case with the open side (where the bobbin is inserted) to the left. Turn the large screw clockwise or to the right to tighten the tension and counterclockwise or to the left to loosen it. Remember the saying "right is tight, left is loose."

You would be wise when manipulating the tension screw to hold the bobbin case over a box lid or open envelope because the tension screw is less than a ¼" in length and is easily unscrewed too far, which may send it flying to some distant place in the room. If this happens get your vacuum cleaner out and put an old nylon stocking over the nozzle. Soon you will have a clean sewing room and your tension screw will be visible on the nylon.

Testing Rotary Bobbin Tension

To test the tension, hold on to the thread and let the bobbin in the bobbin case drop yo-yo fashion. If you do this over and over you will begin to learn what normal tension feels like. The bobbin case should drop 2" to 3" and stop. If it drops more than that, tighten (turn to the right) the tension screw one eighth of a turn and try again. If it drops less than 2" to 3", loosen (turn to left) the screw one eighth of a turn and try again.

Testing Drop-in Bobbin Tension

The tension screw is located alongside a numbered or plus or minus scale. The scale is the same scale used on the needle tension dial. The only way to test the tension of a drop-in bobbin is to tug on the bobbin thread after each minute adjustment of the screw. Read your machine instruction manual to understand how to adjust this kind of bobbin tension.

Heavy Thread and Bobbin Tension

When you use a heavy thread in the bobbin you may either wind the bobbin in the usual way or wind it by hand (see "Heavy Weight

Decorative Threads" in Chapter Three). In either case, the tension screw will need to be adjusted to decrease the amount of tension exerted on the thread. Some threads are so heavy that they will not slide through the tension band even if the screw has been loosened to its maximum. When this is the case, I have had success by removing the heavy thread from under the tension band and simply threading it through the large opening in the bobbin case.

An Exercise in Sewing Machine Tension

Please take time to do the following exercise to better understand your sewing machine tension.

1. Cut eight pieces of medium weight fabric 3" x 8".

2. Choose two spools of machine embroidery thread of the same type and weight, but of two different colors. The threads should stand in contrast to the fabric and to each other.

3. Thread the needle with one spool of thread and the bobbin with the other.

4. Set the sewing machine for a zigzag stitch 4mm wide and 4mm long. Use balanced tensions in the needle and the bobbin.

5. Take two of the eight pieces of fabric and place one on top of the other. Sew a balanced row of stitches down the center of the strip. A balanced stitch locks between the fabrics at both the beginning and the end of each stitch so that only the needle thread is visible on top of the fabric and only the bobbin thread is visible on the underside (Fig. 1.9a).

6. Remove the bobbin case from the sewing machine, pull some thread from the bobbin through the bobbin tension, and note how this feels. Do this several times, trying to learn what normal tension pull feels like.

7. Repeat the first step using two new strips of

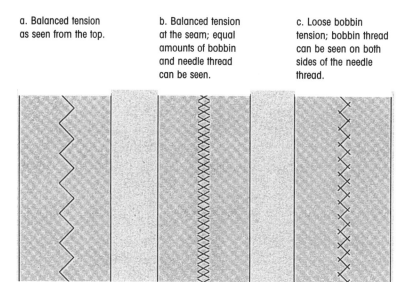

a. Balanced tension as seen from the top.

b. Balanced tension at the seam; equal amounts of bobbin and needle thread can be seen.

c. Loose bobbin tension; bobbin thread can be seen on both sides of the needle thread.

1.9 Balanced versus unbalanced stitches.

fabric. This time open the seam and note that the two colors of thread meet halfway in the center of the seam, a further indication of a balanced stitch (Fig. 1.9b).

8. Next, increase the needle tension by two numbers. Turn the needle tension dial to seven, for example, if your sewing machine is adjusted to perform a balanced stitch at five. Using two more pieces of fabric, stitch a row of 4mm wide zigzag stitches down the center. This time you will see that the bobbin thread has come to the surface so that both the needle thread and the bobbin thread are visible (Fig. 1.9c).

9. Now decrease the needle tension by two numbers. If, for example, a balanced tension is five, decrease the tension to three. Using two more pieces of fabric, stitch a row of 4mm wide zigzag stitches down the center. The surface of the stitching will look normal, but when you look underneath you'll see that the needle thread has been pulled to the back of the fabric.

10. Add these sewn strips to your collection of samples along with a note detailing the exact tension used to sew each strip. I find it helpful to store these in a plastic page for future reference.

Hints

• When the needle thread is pulled to the underside of the fabric the needle tension is loose or the bobbin tension is very tight.

• When the bobbin thread is pulled to the front side of the fabric the needle tension is tight or the bobbin tension is very loose.

CARING FOR YOUR SEWING MACHINE

No chapter on the intricacies of the sewing machine would be complete without advice on its upkeep. Most of the current models on the market today need very little maintenance. Some do not even need any oil. Read the owner's manual, however, and be sure to oil if so directed.

If your machine is older and there are lots of places to put oil and/or grease do it religiously, but be careful not to oil anything until you have removed the dust and lint. Most manuals remind us to unplug the machine and remove the presser foot and needle before cleaning. Clean the feed dogs, the hook area, bobbin case, and bobbin thread monitor with a brush or clean cotton cloth. (Even if your machine does not need any oil it needs to be cleaned.) I remove dust and lint from my machines as I walk by with the vacuum cleaner. Recently my vacuum cleaner repair man showed me an attachment for any vacuum hose. It has several miniature parts, including a brush and a crevice tool which fit into tight spaces and really suck out the dust and lint. Never use a screwdriver or other sharp instrument to remove lint. After cleaning, put a drop of oil in the hook raceway—the movable part of the bobbin area seen after the bobbin case is removed—if directed to do so in the machine manual. A good rule of thumb is to oil any part that moves as long as it is not plastic.

Every machine manufacturer seems to suggest a different frequency for oiling. Their recommendations are based on general sewing time, which allows for pinning and pressing, etc. In machine embroidery often the motor goes fast for long periods of time and so I recommend that you clean and oil your sewing machine after every four hours of embroidery. Clean it more often if the fabric being embroidered is creating a lot of lint.

Even if there is nothing wrong with your machine I suggest that you have it serviced annually to insure that the timing remains accurate, that it is cleaned in all the places you do not usually reach, and that the built-in stitches remain balanced.

In addition to a sewing machine, sewers have an abundance of helpful devices to assist in the ease and fun of machine embroidery. In the next chapter you will read about the most useful of these notions and have a chance to decide which you cannot live without.

Tools of the Trade
Supplies for Machine Embroidery

> *The only time you can't afford to*
> *fail is the last time you try.*
> —Charles Kettering

Most of us like gadgets and machine embroiderers are no exception! Students who come to my studio on a regular basis now bring their sewing machines plus a suitcase. It looks for all the world like they are all moving in.

Although the number of sewing machine accessories is huge, in this chapter I will mention only those supplies I have found to be most useful over the years (Fig. 2.1).

SEWING MACHINE SUPPLIES

THREAD

Thread is your most important asset other than your sewing machine. Start with several spools each of 40 wt rayon and metallic machine embroidery thread. Add to this a spool or two of very fine 60 to 70 wt machine embroidery bobbin thread. Since there is a lot of stress on the bobbin thread in some machine embroidery techniques, the bobbin thread needs to be strong, probably polyester. Also purchase a couple of spools of clear monofilament thread to use in couching threads and applying beads by

machine. Detailed information about machine embroidery thread may be found in Chapter Three: It Takes a Needle and Thread.

NEEDLES

Have a good supply of 8/60 through 18/110 universal point sewing machine needles. The new embroidery needles are excellent for rayon and metallic threads. Twin and triple needles are fun. These needles will get you started,

2.1 Essential sewing machine and machine embroidery supplies.

and you can add to your supply as you go along. You will undoubtedly break more needles doing machine embroidery than you do with regular sewing so buy a couple of extra packages. See Chapter Three for comprehensive needle information and a complete needle chart.

EMBROIDERY SPRING

An embroidery spring performs the same function as a darning foot, forcing the fabric to lay flat and firmly on the bed of the sewing machine at the exact moment a stitch is made. Its benefit is that it allows better visibility while embroidering. The coil that incrementally increases in size fits around the shank of the needle. It cannot be used with a slant needle sewing machine.

SPRING NEEDLE

Spring needles have a spring similar to the embroidery spring built into the needle and function in the same way. These needles are rather expensive, but they are a big help to the embroiderer who needs more tension on the fabric as the stitches are formed. Spring needles allow better visibility than either a darning foot or an embroidery spring. I have found it possible to remove the spring from a worn or damaged needle and reapply it to a new needle.

NEEDLE THREADER

If your machine has a needle threader built in, learn to use it. Machine embroidery threads, especially metallic threads, tend to split just as the needle is being threaded. Purchase a manual threader otherwise.

PRESSER FEET

An embroidery presser foot, an open toe embroidery foot (often called an appliqué foot), a darning foot, and a quilting bar usually come as standard equipment with your sewing machine. If not, you will need to purchase these from your dealer.

For more information on presser feet, review Chapter One.

EXTRA BOBBINS

It is convenient to have a large supply of bobbins because you may want to use many, many colors of thread in one project. Each thread should have its own bobbin because poorly constructed stitches may occur when you use different colors or weights of thread on the same bobbin. For best results, use the bobbin specified by your machine's manufacturer.

EXTRA BOBBIN CASE

In machine embroidery, the bobbin tension is often adjusted to change the texture of the embroidery. Consequently, you may find it easier to have one bobbin case that is used exclusively for regular sewing and one that is readjusted frequently for machine embroidery. Some sewing machine manufacturers carry a special bobbin that accommodates heavier threads; ask your dealer.

LINT BRUSH

Most machines come with a small lint brush. When that wears out, use a one inch paint brush. It will really clean the lint and dust from the bobbin case area.

SEWING MACHINE OIL

Clean out the bobbin area and use oil on the hook raceway following the manufacturer's manual. Use only sewing machine oil, which is a finer grade than ordinary household oil.

SPOOL PIN CAPS

Use a spool pin cap to ensure that the spool of thread stays on the horizontal spool pin. Most machines come with various sizes, but small and large are the most helpful. Use the small size when the spool does not interfere with the thread as it runs through the machine. The large size will save you much frustration if the spool is rough or if the thread saver (the notch in the spool) catches the thread as the machine is running. The large cap is usually larger than the diameter of the thread spool so that the thread glides on the cap and not on the rough spool. This is also useful on a vertical spool pin.

SPOOLS

In addition to regular spools, there is a type of spool called a "snap spool," so named because on each side of the spool is a flange (Fig. 2.2). This is a neat little device to eliminate thread waste and tangling when not in use. Gently ease the flange open to remove the end of the thread. When the work is finished, merely pull the thread into the flange. Closing the flange will secure the thread.

2.2 Spool pin caps ensure that the thread spool stays on the spool pin.

THREAD STAND

A thread stand is a square or round disk with a short metal rod, which acts as a spool pin, positioned vertically in the center. Off to the side is a taller rod, usually around 18" in height, with a hook at the top. The spool of thread is placed over the short rod in the center of the base and the thread is threaded through the hook at the top of the longer rod. Place the thread stand beside the machine to the far right so that you may thread your machine in the usual way after the thread leaves the thread stand. When using a thread stand the thread leaves the cone unencumbered, eliminating any jerking or catching on the spool or cone itself. This is helpful in eliminating thread breakage, especially with metal threads.

SMALL SCREW DRIVER

A small screw driver, which is a standard accessory when you purchase a new machine, is often used to unscrew the needle and to change the bobbin tension. Most machines allow the removal of the ankle, which holds the foot. A small screw driver will help here too.

EMBROIDERY SUPPLIES

The projects further along in this book use many of the supplies listed below (see Fig. 2.1). You will find that they help to make machine embroidery fun and easy.

SEAM RIPPER

A seam ripper with a fine point is essential when stitches must be removed.

IRON

It is essential to press often when machine embroidering. On dense embroidery it is best to press after every row. The Topjet Vario Iron by Passap-USA produces lots of steam and has solved several pucker problems for me. See the Source List in the reference section at the back of the book for additional information.

CHALK

The easiest chalk to use is a powder that is dispensed from a plastic case and leaves a very fine line. Clo-Chalk Marker is an air-erasable white chalk that leaves no greasy residue and disappears in four to five days, or you can iron it away immediately. For more information, see the Source List at the back of the book.

Check all markers on a scrap of the same fabric you are using to be certain that the marker is easily removed and does not damage the fabric.

AIR- AND WATER-REMOVABLE MARKING PENS

Air- and water-removable marking pens, usually violet and blue, respectively, are very useful when transferring a design to fabric. Be sure to try the pen on a sample of the fabric to be embroidered by wetting the mark and waiting up to twenty-four hours for it to disappear. Synthetic fabric is particularly sensitive to the chemicals in these pencils and may "hold on to" the color after the fabric is dry. Refer to Chapter Four for instructions on how to transfer designs from paper to fabric.

Conservationists are not yet sure if these water- and air-removable markers will have a long range effect on fabric. I recently spoke with someone at the Smithsonian in Washington, DC, who said "ask me in fifty years!"

STRAIGHT PINS

Long quilting pins are the most useful. Insert pins horizontally to the presser foot. Do not sew over pins using zigzag stitches, twin needles, or pre-programmed stitches.

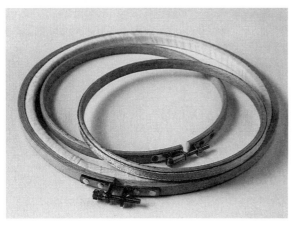

2.3 Machine embroidery hoops come in several sizes.

MACHINE EMBROIDERY HOOPS

Screw-type round wooden machine embroidery hoops 6" and 8" in diameter are the best kind to start with (Fig. 2.3). See "To Hoop or Not to Hoop" in Chapter Four for further information.

EMBROIDERY SCISSORS

These small scissors are needed to cut threads close to the embroidery. Please get yourself a pair

if you do not already have one. Your dressmaking scissors will not do. I recently acquired a pair of Mundial 4½" Threadclips. They are comfortable to hold and cut threads close to the fabric. See the Source List at the back of the book for additional information.

RULER

You will need a ruler 12" to 15" long, preferably of clear plastic, to make a guideline on some projects that require a straight line for stitching.

TWEEZERS

Tweezers make it easy to remove stray threads and lint from the bobbin case area. I often use them to remove tear away stabilizer after stitching.

Tweezers are also useful when applying beads by machine. Gripping the bead with the tweezers and threading the bead on the needle is often less cumbersome than doing it by hand.

TAPE MEASURE

I prefer a fabric or paper tape measure instead of a metal one. The fabric tape measure is easier to carry with my sewing supplies and is more useful when measuring curves and angles.

FRAY PREVENTER

Fray preventer is a colorless solution in a plastic squeeze bottle that is applied to fabrics and threads to eliminate fraying or unraveling. The solution is permanent through many washings. It is also good for controlling pantyhose runs.

PLASTIC INSERT PAGES

Use plastic insert pages to preserve stitch samples, experimental stitching, and scraps of finished projects for future reference. Purchase plastic insert pages at your local stationery store.

2.4 Stabilizers come in a variety of formats, including fusible, sewable, iron-on, liquid, and many more.

STABILIZERS

A stabilizer, sometimes called a backing, forms an unstretchable surface that allows the embroidery stitches to lay flat and undisturbed on the surface of the fabric (Fig. 2.4). Stabilizers enhance the appearance and prolong the life of decorated fabric. Stretch and woven fabrics are most commonly used when machine embroidering. Both types of fabric have different amounts of stretch and give. When machine embroidering, it is important to stitch into a stable fabric. Tightly woven twill, for example, can be hooped and embroidered with no stabilizer, but if a loosely woven fabric or one that is highly stretchable is stitched into, the stitches will be distorted. Distorted stitches tend to pull the threads in the fabric together, causing puckering and distortion of the weave of the fabric.

A stabilizer also helps prevent skipped stitches and thread wear, which results in the needle thread breaking.

It is wise to use a stabilizer for machine embroidery, appliqué, cutwork, and monogramming. Refer to Chapter Four to learn all about the different types of stabilizers available and how to use them.

FABRICS FOR MACHINE EMBROIDERY

I have never seen a fabric that I would not use for machine embroidery. The most difficult fabric to embellish would be one with a high pile, and even this can be surmounted if the fabric is hooped with a piece of tissue paper over the top that is then torn away after stitching. Any fabric that inspires you is fair game; just remember to hoop and stabilize loosely woven fabric. Your stash of fabrics is a fun part of machine embroidery. You will find solid color fabric the most useful. Often I have been referred to, however, as the queen of bold ugly fabrics because they offer some of the most amazing design possibilities.

FABRIC PAINTS AND BEADS

Go for it! Both paint and beads add immensely to some embroideries. If you have never used fabric paint purchase a half-dozen colors and some medium weight white fabric and a sponge. Save some trays from the meat counter or a supermarket to blend paints into unique colors.

As far as beads are concerned, just start collecting. Try to be attracted only to beads with a hole large enough to accommodate a 70/10 needle. The length of the bead is also important because the shaft of the needle widens as it blends into the shank. Often beads will break if the length of the bead interferes with the needle's descent to meet the bobbin thread.

Specific ideas using beads and fabric paint in machine embroidery are included in Chapter Six.

Only two major supplies need further explanation. Machine embroidery thread and sewing machine needles. Most sewers would agree with me that thread is the lifeblood of embroidery. Read on to learn the tricks of embroidering with everything from cotton to shiny rayon to flashy metallics.

It Takes a Needle and Thread

The Sparkle and Life of Machine Embroidery

> *It's a funny thing about life: if you refuse to accept anything but the very best you will very often get it.*
> —W. Somerset Maugham

Most books about machine embroidery on the market today seem to skim over the very exciting subject of machine embroidery thread. Over the years I've worked with literally hundreds of different kinds of threads and I've found that even if you don't have a state-of-the-art sewing machine, the thread you choose may be all you need to make your embroidery alive and exciting.

MACHINE EMBROIDERY THREAD

How do machine embroidery threads differ from garment construction threads? Let me begin by saying that not all threads are created equal. Machine embroidery threads and garment construction threads are two peas in different pods. They are manufactured differently for two different purposes.

THREAD PLY

Machine embroidery thread is always two ply so that the thread rests smoothly on the fabric (Fig. 3.1). This means that it is not manufactured for strength, since two strands of thread twisted together do not create a strong thread. Some garment construction thread is also two ply. It is usually of very poor quality and made of short staples called fibers that are plied together. It is often bumpy, not very strong, and of poor color quality as well.

3.1 Unlike most garment construction threads, machine embroidery thread is always two ply.

Most garment construction thread is three ply, meaning that three strands are twisted together. These three tightly twisted strands lend each other strength when they are tugged. Such strength is not necessary for machine embroidery thread since its purpose is to embellish the fabric, not hold it together.

THREAD WEIGHT

If a machine embroidery spool reads 50/2 it is a 50 wt (weight) thread, meaning that fifty hanks of 840 yards each equal one pound. A 40 wt thread means that forty hanks of 840 yards each equal one pound. The number 2 refers to the number of plies twisted together to form one strand of thread. The finer the thread the higher the number. A 60 wt machine embroidery thread, for example, is finer than a 50 wt machine embroidery thread. But be aware that a 50 wt machine embroidery thread is not the same weight as a 50 wt garment construction thread.

They are different because their methods of construction differ. A single ply of machine embroidery thread is first given a left hand or **S** twist with twenty to thirty twists per inch. Then two plies of thread, each having been given a left (**S**) twist, are twisted to the right, forming a **Z** twist. The change in twist direction helps avoid thread kinks while giving the thread strength and decreasing the possibility of untwisting. Garment construction threads, on the other hand, are manufactured in the opposite manner, first being **Z** twisted and then **S** twisted.

The amount of twist given a thread is one component in determining its color, strength, and quality. Tightly twisted threads lay flatter and wear better.

3.2 The thread nap lays in one direction

THREAD NAP

Nap is described in Webster's Dictionary as a short fiber on the surface which lays smoothly in one direction (Fig. 3.2). The nap of all sewing machine thread, whether it be garment construction or machine embroidery thread, is laying down as it comes off the spool. This is important in machine embroidery for two reasons. The first is that more light is reflected from the thread when the nap is laying down. Shiny threads will loose some shine if they are stitched in the opposite direction. The second reason is that the thread will not wear as well if the nap of the thread is up.

Often we may wind thread on to a bobbin and then sew with the bobbin on the spool pin. Consequently, the thread is being stitched against its nap. So if you are using a bobbin on your spool holder and the thread is breaking, you know why! To solve this problem, wind the thread from its original spool on to a bobbin and

then wind the bobbin thread on to a second bobbin for embroidery use.

THREAD DYE

Today's range of thread colors is immense and allows the embroiderer unlimited possibilities, especially in light of the fact that when you machine embroider, you can use two threads in the needle and three hundred or more built-in machine embroidery patterns. When choosing a thread color, it is always wise to remember that threads look lighter after they are sewn, unless they are used to stitch an area of one solid color.

Today's dye houses produce permanent, even, thread color that we can depend on time after time. The process used for dyeing thread today is complex but accurate and permanent. The complexity comes from our responsibility to protect the environment and our need to produce the same color time after time.

I want to caution you, however, that there is a difference between the dye running and the over dye of the thread bleeding. Over dye of thread bleeding happens most often in dark shades such as black, red, navy, forest green, and deep violet. Because these shades require a lot of chemical in the dye bath to reach the correct intensity of color, the dye house will add extra pigment to the dye bath. When the thread is rinsed some dark colors do not rid themselves of the excess dye, known as the over dye. So during the first laundering you may see some crocking, which is the imparting of dye to surrounding fabric. This need not be a disaster. Simply continue rinsing the article until all the over dye has been removed. A word of caution—keep rinsing until all of the over dye is removed. If the embroidered article is allowed to dry while crocking is still occurring, the crocked color will be permanent in the embellished article. When you believe that all of the over dye has been removed, roll the item in a towel to remove the excess water and lay the article flat to dry.

Highly pigmented thread colors also pose another challenge. Since these threads contain more chemical dye than lighter colors they may be weakened by the dye. Be sure highly pigmented threads have a large enough needle to protect them from fraying and breaking during sewing.

PARALLEL- AND CROSS-WOUND SPOOLS

Thread is wound on a spool in two different ways, parallel- and cross-wound. Parallel-wound thread is wound so that each row encircling the spool is one thread thickness below the previous row (Fig. 3.3a). The thread unwinds from the spool one row at a time from the top to the bottom of the spool and then back to the top again. Parallel-wound spools run more smoothly in the vertical position. Cross-wound spools are wound in a **Z** pattern up and down the spool (Fig. 3.3b). Many cross-wound spools are made of paper board and are called cop spools. Cross-wound spools are manufactured to run from the horizontal position on the spool pin or from a thread stand.

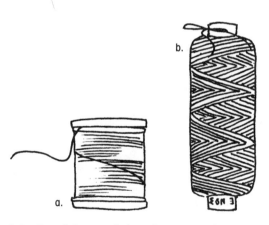

3.3a. Parallel-wound thread on a spool.
3.3b. Cross-wound thread on a spool.

TYPES OF MACHINE EMBROIDERY THREAD

Although it is tempting to use your old garment construction thread, I give you permission right now to throw it all over your shoulder and have fun choosing interesting, unusual embroidery threads that will immediately improve the quality of your work. But if you still need to be convinced of the difference between threads, try sewing a

sample using a 3–4mm wide satin stitch. Stitch a row using garment construction threads you have on hand. Now stitch several rows in the same satin stitch with machine embroidery rayon and metallic threads. You will notice that the machine embroidery threads lay flatter on the surface of the fabric and do a better job of covering the area. In addition to giving your stitches a more elegant look, embroidery thread gives your stitches a higher sheen. Additionally, metallic threads give your stitches a highly reflective quality.

Now let's take a walk down Thread Lane together. Let me warn you though, there are all types of wonderful detours. Threads are the magic of your embroidery and will give your embroidery a unique character.

Rayon Thread

In most cases rayon thread is 100% viscose rayon, a synthetic fiber made from cellulose that is chemically treated and forced through a spinneret. The process of forcing the viscose through the spinneret imitates how the silkworm spins its thread. You can understand, then, why viscose rayon is often called artificial silk. A more modern process allows air to compress the thread together, but the silky effect remains the same.

Viscose rayon is a shiny, lustrous thread, a fact which will help you to spot it at your local fabric and sewing machine store. Rayon comes in 30 and 40 wts, which are very fine threads. Size 30 wt requires slightly less needle tension than 40 wt.

Not all brands of machine embroidery rayon thread are of good quality. Look for an evenly colored rayon thread that holds its twist off the spool. The color range should have at least three values to each shade or tint. The tighter the twist (the higher the number of twists), the darker in color the thread appears because the twists break up the reflective surface of the thread.

Because 40 wt rayon is fine it also contributes to the smoothness of your embroidery stitch. This brings clarity and good definition to stitching, particularly when used with the built-in patterns of your sewing machine. Rayon machine embroidery threads are available in a range of approximately three hundred colors, with several values of each color. Rayon also comes in ombre colors, which vary, for example, from white to a tinge of pink to light pink to a deep pink and back to white. It is common to find a dozen or more colors in ombre. Next are the variegated colors, which are very interesting and fun. You will find variegated spools in combinations such as red, green, blue, and yellow; gold, black, and red; and grass green, lavender, and gold (a few of my favorites).

Rayon threads are easy to care for. They can be washed in hot water up to 203 degrees Fahrenheit without changing color or shine. They can safely be put in the dryer and can be dry cleaned. Just don't bleach them.

Rayon threads are slippery and tend to slide off the spool, particularly the 1000 yard spools. If you have this trouble place your hands on either end of the spool and push both ends of thread toward the center. This causes the thread to be more compact, decreasing slippage. You may also use an old nylon stocking sewn to fit the spool to hold the threads on the spool while stitching. A third trick is to use a parallel or horizontal spool holder.

Rayon threads are used in machine embroidery when doing appliqué, using built-in program stitches, couching other threads, doing free motion embroidery, and doing thread painting. Rayon threads are also elegant in the needles and loopers of the serger. In other words, rayon machine embroidery thread is very versatile and there is no end to your creativity with it!

To use rayon thread successfully, keep the following points in mind.

- Use a number 90/14 universal or sharp sewing machine needle (not a ball point), or an 80/12–90/14 top stitching needle, or an 80/12–90/14 machine embroidery needle.

- Start stitching slowly.

- If you are stitching solid, dense stitches use a stabilizer and or a hoop to prevent puckering. Remember to press with an iron frequently.

- Loosen the needle tension by decreasing the tension dial one number.

- In the bobbin, use a machine embroidery thread that is specifically designed for bobbin use. Madeira's Bobbinfil is a good example (see the Source List at the back of the book for additional information).

- If your needle thread is breaking, tape a tapestry needle to the left of the vertical spool pin and as the thread leaves the spool pin, thread it through the needle. This keeps the thread at an even height as it leaves the spool and prevents it from getting caught and wound around the spool pin.

- You can also prevent thread breakage by putting the spool of thread in a cup behind the sewing machine and threading the machine as usual with the thread passing in front of the spool pin.

- Use a thread stand.

- Start each project with a new needle.

- Check to make sure that the hole in the throat plate is smooth. If you have broken several needles they have undoubtedly marred the throat plate, making it rough and abrasive to decorative thread. The solution is to take a pumice cloth and rub the rough area until it is smooth. If this fails, a new throat plate is not very expensive.

If you find that you are having difficulty stitching with any of the decorative threads turn to Chapter Eight: When Things Go Wrong.

Silk Thread

Silk embroidery thread is very luxurious and naturally light reflective. The silk machine embroidery thread on the market today is all three ply. This means it is stronger than most other embroidery threads. The color range is limited, however, to approximately thirty colors. Silk thread tends to be pricey and so unless you are working on a piece to be passed on through the generations, rayon or acrylic thread may suit your purpose as well or even better. Silk thread, however, will make built-in stitches and free motion work look glorious. Bold rows of stitching with silk thread (at least a 1.5mm wide satin stitch) will act as a resist when painting on silk fabric. Although a resist is usually a chemical that prevents paint from bleeding beyond it, using silk thread as a resist could have some fascinating results.

Silk thread is available in 50 and 30 wts as well as buttonhole twist, which is an extra heavy, tightly twisted thread used originally for hand sewn buttonholes. Buttonhole twist is suitable for topstitching and decorative stitches that are open and do not include satin stitch. Some of the maxi patterns on the current model machines that only use straight stitch are a perfect use for buttonhole twist.

Silk embroidery floss is supplied in more than one hundred colors. It works wonderfully in the bobbin of the sewing machine or laid on top of the fabric and stitched over with a built-in pattern. This is called couching, which I discuss in detail in Chapter Seven.

Metallic Thread

Many of the same things that were said about rayon thread can be said about metallic thread. Metallic thread is most often 40 wt, although there are many beautiful metallic threads in 30 and 20 wt, both of which are heavier than 40 wt. Metallic thread is available in more than one hundred colors.

Look for metallic thread in solid colors as well as combinations such as gold, pink, blue, and silver; gold, red, green, and turquoise; black and gold; and black and silver. A new metallic thread that recently entered the market is called Jewel. It has a black undertone with colored metallics, making it especially suitable for stitching black and denim fabrics.

Metallics catch your eye, they dazzle you and those around you. Some machine embroidery metal threads actually have about five percent gold or silver in them. Metallics however, are generally non-metal threads and are predominately strong films of plastic and/or polyester. They are vacuum plated with aluminum and then either solution coated with a colored cover coat or laminated to another layer of thin film to make a sandwich that protects the metallic coat from wear. This thin film is coated with transparent dyes to give various colors.

With just a few bits of advice you will enjoy sewing with these uniquely sparkling threads. All the cautions given in using rayon thread apply to metallic threads, plus the following:

• You may need to switch to a larger needle (100/16) when you first begin using metallics to avoid thread breakage.

• Sew slowly without fast starts or stops. If your sewing machine seems to jerk the thread as it comes off the spool, place the spool on a thread stand or in a cup behind your sewing machine and then thread it in the normal way.

• Use a needle threader when threading the machine. Metallic threads tend to split during threading.

• Try using machine embroidery needles. These new needles are specially crafted to protect decorative threads. Refer back to Chapter Two: Tools of the Trade for more information about these needles.

Polyester Thread

Polyester thread looks like rayon thread and is used in a similar manner. The color range is much narrower than rayon thread, approximately one hundred twenty colors compared with rayon's three hundred colors. The most important factor in your decision to use polyester decorative machine embroidery thread over rayon thread is its strength. Polyester thread is about four times stronger than rayon thread and is abrasion resistant. Polyester is a man-made thread produced in much the same way as rayon. It too is forced through a spinneret or air compressed. Polyester thread is made of petroleum chemicals and combined with ethylene glycol. Polyester has high colorfastness and, unlike rayon, it is bleachable. Polyester threads require slightly more needle tension than rayon threads. Be careful, however, not to put excess tension on polyester thread as it has a better memory, meaning that it has a natural tendency to return to its original length when tension is released. Latent puckering may occur in the decorated fabric after the hoop is removed if excess tension is used at the time of embroidery. This kind of puckering is impossible to remove even with an iron and steam.

Acrylic Thread

Acrylic fibers are made of coal, air, water, petroleum, and limestone. Combined they form polyacrylonitrile. Since it is a man-made fiber, acrylic is also forced through a spinneret or is air compressed to form a thread. Acrylic thread is stronger than rayon and polyester, but it is sensitive to heat. The fiber softens even at the low temperatures used in the iron or the clothes dryer. Acrylic fibers do not stretch or shrink. They take dye well, especially bold bright colors. Acrylic 50 wt, two ply thread for machine embroidery is available in fifty-four colors.

Cotton Thread

Cotton is the most important natural fiber we have and its use goes back to 3000 BC in India and possibly even to 1,200 BC in Egypt. One hundred percent cotton machine embroidery threads are wonderful fibers to use. High quality thread is manufactured of the finest Egyptian cotton, which goes through the processes of carding, combing, drawing, and roving, and is finally spun into thread. Next it is mercerized, which involves treating the cotton with caustic soda to add strength and luster while removing bumps from the thread. Mercerization also gives cotton more absorbent qualities.

Because cotton is made of cellulose and is formed in minute particles the fiber is porous and can readily absorb water. The more water it absorbs (up to 20%) the stronger cotton is. If there is too much moisture, however, some of cotton's elasticity is lost.

The processes of carding through mercerization all happen before the cotton machine embroidery thread reaches the dye house, where it easily takes on a wonderful range of color. With nearly two hundred colors, its range is almost as wide as rayon's. I choose cotton embroidery threads when the embroidery or ground fabric demands a matte finish. Good quality cotton

threads have a surprisingly high luster and are very rich looking.

If your cotton threads seem to break easily it is probably because the air in your house is dry and they have lost some of their moisture content. There are a few tricks which help to restore the moisture, such as leaving the spool of thread in the refrigerator for a couple of days. Recently someone told me that she did not have a couple of days to wait for the moisture content to increase, so she steamed the spool on a rack over boiling water. Another instant trick may simply be to discard the top layer of thread on the spool. The underlayer may have been protected enough to have kept its natural moisture. Save the discarded thread in your orts pile.

Orts, by the way, is a real word, although my students have often accused me of making it up! Webster's Dictionary defines orts as the leavings, or sweepings; it does say garbage, but we know better! Orts are our waste threads and in my studio they land on the floor and then are swept up and saved so that they can be easily couched to another fiber.

Keep in mind that you may combine cotton embroidery threads with rayon and/or metallic threads to add different textures and light reflection in your embroidery. This may be the secret to making your embroidery a successful design. Cotton threads are commonly available in three weights for machine embroidery. The heaviest thread, 30 wt, fills built-in stitches well. A finer, thinner thread, 50 wt produces wonderful detail. I often use 50 wt cotton even though I have to take a few more stitches than I would if I were using the 30 wt. Because I cover less ground with each stitch, I am able to make more accurate decisions about where and what to stitch next. The finest, 80 wt, is very fine and used for lace making and heirloom sewing and embroidery on both the sewing machine and serger.

Invisible Nylon Thread

Commonly referred to as Wonderthread or Monofil, this fine transparent nylon thread can be used in both the needle and the bobbin of the sewing machine. It is usually available in both clear and smoke. Use the clear for white and pastel color fabric. Use smoke for all strong color fabrics (red, black, etc.). Use this thread when you do not want the stitching to show in machine quilting, appliqué, blind hems, couching of heavy threads, and when sewing beads by machine.

A word of caution: Only fill plastic bobbins half full of invisible thread. Since it is so fine, a tremendous amount will fit on a bobbin, which causes so much pressure that the plastic bobbin may fracture! When using monofilament thread decrease the needle tension by one number to prevent stretching of the thread.

Wool and Acrylic Thread

This thread creates a new look in machine embroidery. Its brand names are Lanny, Burmilana, and Renaissance thread. It is 30% wool and 70% acrylic. It is washable and dry cleanable. Wool threads always produce a lot of lint in the bobbin case area, so be sure to brush it out frequently. Use a large needle with this variety of thread (110/18) and be sure to decrease the needle tension by at least one number. This thread can be used with large straight stitches (3.5 or larger), open decorative stitches, and in free motion embroidery. Avoid using wool and acrylic thread in satin stitches. Bargello, needlepoint, and crewel embroidery by machine are handsome with this thread. See the "Zig and Zag Bargello Coin Purse" and "Machine Crewelled Mums" in Chapter Six, two projects made with wool and acrylic threads.

With a little practice it is amazing how much the free motion embroidery looks like hand done crewel embroidery.

Knitting Elastic

Knitting elastic used in the bobbin of the sewing machine is very interesting. Wind the bobbin in the usual way and loosen the bobbin tension so that it feeds through the bobbin smoothly. On some machines you may get good results by bypassing the bobbin tension all together. Set your machine with a long and wide zigzag or long straight stitch and sew rows 1½"

apart. When you are finished the fabric will automatically gather up. Knitting elastic in the bobbin can also be used in free motion embroidery stitched randomly.

Heavy Weight Decorative Threads

Heavy weight threads can be used in two ways in your sewing machine. The first method involves couching, which Webster's Dictionary defines as fastening one working thread to the ground fabric by making stitches over it with another thread. Couching with the sewing machine is done by laying one thread on the ground fabric and securing it in place with a straight stitch or a built-in pre-programmed pattern or zigzag stitch. Couching can be done either with the presser foot and feed dogs in use or in the free motion embroidery mode. Couching is very effective using thread, yarn, braid, or ribbon which is too heavy to run through the bobbin. Several projects in Chapter Seven use this technique.

The second use for heavy decorative threads is to wind them in the bobbin. Most of the time heavy threads can be wound to a regular sewing machine bobbin in the usual way. If the thread is too heavy to gracefully go through the regular winding route it can be wound by hand.

When using heavy threads in the bobbin, place the fabric to be embroidered upside down on the bed of the sewing machine. The top thread is now seen on the wrong side of the fabric and the heavy thread on the right side of the fabric.

Bobbin Threads

Both rayon and metallic threads can be used in the bobbin of your sewing machine although it is more economical to use these decorative threads in the needle only when the underside stitching does not show. Some difficulty may arise with a front loading or oscillating bobbin if rayon or metallic threads are used. This type of bobbin tends to take a twist forward as the machine stops. When this happens the thread is no longer being taken up by the stitches and may come unwound from the bobbin. This unwound thread tends to tangle and when you begin sewing again the thread may break. To avoid this do not fill a bobbin with rayon or metallic thread more than three quarters full. Begin and finish sewing slowly.

You can avoid this problem altogether by using a thread in the bobbin made especially for machine embroidery. Bobbin threads made especially for machine embroidery are light weight, 70 or 80 wt, and they are strong, usually made of 100% polyester. The extra strength of the polyester helps the thread resist being pulled to the surface by the needle thread. Because the polyester thread is strong the bobbin thread is less likely to break.

Both the strength and the light weight of these bobbin threads are assets in machine embroidery. The light weight thread allows you to wind many more yards on the bobbin at once. This decreases the number of times you need to fill a bobbin while working on a project. I usually fill about six bobbins at a time; then I have this task out of the way and I can concentrate on the fun part.

HEAVY WEIGHT THREADS FOR COUCHING AND BOBBIN USE

NAME	DESCRIPTION	COLORS	PLY	BOBBIN	COUCHED	COMMENT
Decor 6	Heavy 100% Viscose Rayon	40		yes	yes	Can be used in needle for straight stitch. Use 110/18 needle. Use with pre-programmed stitches in the bobbin.
Tinsel Thread	Polymide	12	1 ply	yes	yes	Use with pre-programmed stitches in the needle.
Glamour	65% Viscose 35% Polyester Metallic	25		yes	yes	Metallic heavy weight easy to use in bobbin.
Metallic Braid	Viscose Polymide	12		only 2mm width	yes	Use monofilament to couch.
Decora	100% Rayon	80	2 ply 4 strand	yes	yes	Very heavy; only use with open zigzag stitches in the bobbin.
Silk Embroidery Floss	100% Silk	107	2 ply 5 strand	yes	yes	Excellent in bobbin.
Cotton Embroidery Floss	100% Cotton	330	2 ply 6 strand	yes	yes	Excellent in bobbin.
Fiesta Craft Thread	100% Polyester	12		no	yes	Unusual finished product with threads hanging.
Ribbon Floss	Metallic and Rayon	46		yes	yes	Similar use as metallic braid.
Knitting Elastic	Elastic and nylon	2		yes	yes	After release from hoop fabric gathers.

SEWING MACHINE NEEDLES

I remember that when my mother purchased a new sewing machine, she came home with the machine, which had a needle in it, and began to sew. It was only when the needle broke that she ran to her dealer for another. She probably bought just one needle and came home to continue sewing a project.

One of my students recently broke a needle in class and I overheard her say "Oh darn, I was going to will that needle to my granddaughter!" She said that just to get my goat (I wonder where that saying came from) because I have a passion for using the right needle for the job. A lot has changed about sewing since our mothers and grandmothers had their first machines. Fabrics and threads have been developed that were not even dreamed of then and we are lucky to have them. Of course, these vast choices mean that we need to know what thread and needle and fabric together produce the best stitch.

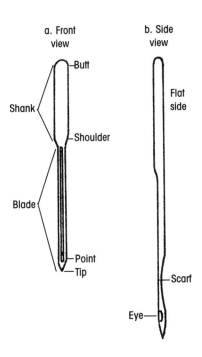

3.4 The parts of a sewing machine needle.

NEEDLE STRENGTH AND QUALITY

Since machine embroidery threads are manufactured to embellish the fabric only, the embroiderer depends on the needle to protect the thread during stitching. The needle must forge a hole large enough to allow the thread to go through the layers of fabric—and perhaps layers of already embroidered thread—without wear. Wear on the thread causes the thread to fray, weaken, or break. Change to the next larger size needle if the thread frays or breaks, but be aware that even if the worn thread does not break during stitching it will still produce an inferior embroidery that will not wear well over the years.

> ### Hint
>
> Fabric stabilization in machine embroidery, especially free motion embroidery, is a very important factor in thread wear and needle size. The more secure and taut the ground fabric, the less the needle size is affected. Please read further about stabilizers and machine embroidery hoops in Chapter Four: Before You Begin.

I am not going to tell you how many years ago, but I remember my home economics teacher telling our class that needle size is determined by the weight and number of layers of fabric to be stitched through. Thread size and type weren't factors because we were just using "sewing thread." Even today some needle manufacturers give guidelines for needle size according to fabric weight. In machine embroidery we still consider the type and weight of fabric to be used, but other factors are even more critical. In order to choose the correct needle size and point type it helps to know the following:

- Needle size is the diameter of the blade portion of the needle.

- Needle size is primarily determined by the thread size or weight.

- The heavier or more fragile the thread, the larger the needle size.

- Choose the needle point type in relation to the weight and density of the weave of the fabric.

- Always use the proper needle for the make and model machine. If you are unsure, check your sewing machine manual or call your dealer.

European needles are measured in tenths of a millimeter and range in size from 60 to 120. Equivalent American needle sizes are listed in the following chart.

American	8	9	10	11	12	14	16	18	20
European	60	65	70	75	80	90	100	110	120

The higher the number in either American or European needles the larger the diameter of the needle blade and eye size. Often a needle size is written 60/8. The 60 is the equivalent European size and 8 is the American size. The size of each needle is marked on the round portion of the needle shaft. Those with young eyes will have no trouble reading the numbers, while the rest of us will find a small magnifying glass a big help. Some needle manufacturers have built into the plastic storage box a window that magnifies the shaft end of the needle and allows easy readability of the sizes.

Hint

The sewing machine needle has three functions:

- First, to penetrate the fabric.
- Second, to bring the thread through the fabric to meet the hook and bobbin thread.
- Third, to protect the thread during the stitch forming process.

The point and taper of the needle varies with the type of fabric and thread used. Needles are manufactured with four basic point types:

Universal	Ball point	Sharp	Cutting
normal	light	acute	piercing
round		round	

The quality of the stitch is dramatically affected by the quality of the needle used. Quality needles are made in both the United States and Europe. Today needle making is an automated process of twenty-five to thirty steps. Needles are made of stainless steel shaped into wire, then cut, ground, hardened, and chemically treated for smoothness. Then they are straightened and electroplated. These high quality needles magnify your sewing machine's ability to form a perfect stitch. Piercing the fabric at just the right spot, snatching the bobbin thread from the hook and pulling the two threads tight to the fabric requires a precision instrument.

Machine embroidery, particularly free motion embroidery, amplifies stress on the needle because the thread is pulled in all directions without the protection of the presser foot. If the needle is not strong enough it will shatter, or bend so much that the bobbin hook is not able to snatch the top thread. This would result in a skipped stitch. A poor quality needle may bend so much in the direction of the stitching that it runs into the throat plate, denting the plate and causing the needle to break.

There are a large variety of needles available to the home sewer. The following list will help you select the correct needle for each purpose.

- Machine embroidery
- Quilting
- Leather
- Pintucking
- Hemstitching/heirloom embroidery
- Denim
- Knits
- Double and triple needles for multiple rows of decorative stitching
- Self-threading needles/handicap
- Spring needles to assist in free motion embroidery

- Sharp needles (the kind our grandmothers used)
- Universal needles used for both knits and woven fabric
- Topstitching
- Ball point (for knits)

SEWING MACHINE NEEDLE CHART

KIND OF NEEDLE ARTICLE NUMBER PICTURE	SIZES	POINT TYPE	SCARF	EYE	USES
Universal Point 130/705 H	8/60 to 20/120	Semi-ball	Regular	Regular	For woven and tightly knit fabric, especially suitable for zigzag stitch.
Blue Shank Stretch 130/705 HS	11/75 and 14/90 only	Medium ball point	Modified	Large	Knits, synthetics that resist needle penetration or are highly elastic; monograms, machine embroidery. Slides between fibers instead of piercing. Has a flatter blade so that it goes closer to the sewing machine hook and picks up bobbin thread more easily.
Ball Point 130/705 SUK	10/70 to 18/110	Medium ball point	Regular	Regular	Coarse knit fabrics.
130/705 HSES		Light ball point	Regular	Regular	For loosely woven fabrics and machine embroidery.
130/705 H-SKF	10/70 to 18/110	Heavy ball point	Regular	Regular	Industrial use; high speed sewing on loose woven fabrics and knits.
Sharp-Microtex Violet Shank 130/705 H-M	8/60 to 14/90	Acute sharp point; gradual flowing tapered blade.	Regular	Regular	For micro-fibers, silks, fine tightly woven fabrics. Micro-fabrics demand a needle free of burrs or rough edges. Check needle point frequently.
Quilting and Patchwork Green Shank 130/705 H-Q	11/75 and 14/90	Very sharp or ball point; even taper to point.	Regular	Regular	Penetrates several layers of fabric and batting easily. Avoids damage to fabric because of tapered blade.

continued

SEWING MACHINE NEEDLE CHART (Continued)

KIND OF NEEDLE ARTICLE NUMBER PICTURE	SIZES	POINT TYPE	SCARF	EYE	USES
Embroidery Schmetz Red Shank 130/705 H-E	11/75 and 14/90	Slightly rounded (SES)	Large eye; larger groove.	Large eye; larger groove.	Special needle for machine embroidery; enables the needle to form a better loop, which reduces risk of skipped stitch. Use when doing monograms, machine embroidery. Use with rayon, metallic, and heavy threads.
Metafil / Sullivans 11120	12/80 only				
Jeans or Denim 130/705 H-J	10/70 to 18/110	Acute sharp	Regular	Regular	Pierces heavy fabric easily; sharp point prevents needle deflection and ensures straight even stitches.
Leather 130/705 H-LL	10/70 to 20/120	Sharp wedge for cutting	Regular	Regular	Used for leather and suede; pierces leather at a slight angle. Holes close after each stitch is complete. Not good for ultra-suede, plastic, oil cloth, or other synthetic materials because it leaves too large a hole.
130/705 H-PCL	12/80 to 18/110	Narrow wedge point with left twist groove below eye	Regular	Regular	For imitation leather, ultra-suede, plastic sheeting, and oil cloth. Leaves a smaller hole and stronger stitch.
Basting 130/705 RH	12/80 and 14/90	Normal round	Regular	Two eyes, one above other.	Called "the magic needle"; thread lower eye for regular sewing and thread upper eye for basting; use blind stitch setting. Stitch forms only on the zag of the blind stitch; skips all other stitches.
Handicap 130/705 H	12/80 and 14/90	Universal	Regular	Slotted eye	Slot near eye for easier threading; slot weakens needle. Sew more slowly.
130 N	10/70 to 18/110	Normal round point	Regular	Long eye	Similar to topstitch needle except for point. Used to topstitch buttonhole silk or metallics.

continued

SEWING MACHINE NEEDLE CHART *(Continued)*

KIND OF NEEDLE ARTICLE NUMBER PICTURE	SIZES	POINT TYPE	SCARF	EYE	USES
Topstitch 130/705 H	12/80 to 18/110	Sharper than universal	Regular	Regular	For topstitch on tightly woven fabrics. Large eye protects thread from fraying during stitching. Helpful for embroidery using rayon or metallic threads.
Double or Twin 130/705 HZWI	1.6/80 2.0/80 2.5/80 3.0/90 4.0/80 4.0/90 4.0/100 6.0/100	Universal	Regular	Regular	For all double and twin needles use the hand wheel through one complete stitch to ensure that the needles do not hit the throat plate. Twin needles create two parallel rows of stitching, which are ideal for pin tucking. First size number indicates distance between the needles in mm; second number indicates needle size. Thread two top threads on separate sides of tension disks. Activate twin needle key.
Double or Twin Embroidery 130/705 HZWI	2.0/75 3.0/75	Sharp	More pronounced	Large	Accommodates metallics and specialty threads for sewing without fraying thread.
Triple 130/705 HDRI	2.5/80 3.0/80	Normal round point	Regular	Regular	Stitches three rows simultaneously; single bobbin thread. For straight stitching or zigzag. Check that the hole in the throat plate is wide enough to accommodate swing of needle.
Wing or Hemstitch 130/705 WING	100 and 120	Sharp	Flat wide sides along length of blade	Regular	For decorative holes on tightly woven fine fabric. Heirloom sewing and entredeux trim. Use with natural fibers for best results.
Double Wing 130/705 HZWING	100	Sharp and Universal	Winged and long	Regular	Produces a single row of straight stitches and a second row with holes. Use with natural fibers.
Round Shank 287 WH/1738	8/60 to 16/110	Normal round	Regular	Regular	Shank end is round for various older home sewing machines.

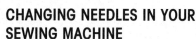

CHANGING NEEDLES IN YOUR SEWING MACHINE

Today's fabrics commonly have a glaze finish that dulls needles easily. Metallic threads, synthetic fibers, and stabilizers made of paper dull needles as well. I tell my students to change to a new needle at the beginning of each project and after four to six hours of sewing.

Before changing a needle read the manufacturer's instruction book for your sewing machine. Always begin by turning the sewing machine off and raising the needle to its highest position. Care must be taken to examine the needle. Run your fingers over the shaft and point. The needle should feel smooth and free of burrs. Hold it up in the light to make sure it is straight. Note that the heavy base of the needle (the shaft) has a round side and a flat side. (If you find a needle that has a completely round shaft it is for industrial sewing machines or some sergers.) Insert the needle into the machine with the flat side away from you or as your sewing machine manual directs. (A few older model machines require the flat side to face left.)

Be sure to insert the needle all the way into the needle clamp mechanism, then tighten the screw. If the needle is inserted backwards no loop will be formed for the bobbin thread and hook to snatch. Consequently, no stitches will be sewn. If the needle is not inserted all the way up into the needle clamp, only some of the stitches will be formed, resulting in skipped stitches.

Now that you have gathered all of your supplies and know the ins and outs of your sewing machine, we are ready to transfer a design to fabric and begin embroidering.

4 | *Chapter Four*

Before You Begin
The Basics of Machine Embroidery

Unless you try to do something beyond what you have already mastered you will never grow.
—Ronald E. Osborn

Learning to embroider with the right equipment is just the beginning of many hours of enjoyment. Read on to learn how to transfer designs to fabric, stabilize fabric, and execute the two methods of embroidery.

TRANSFERRING A DESIGN FROM PAPER TO FABRIC

Designs have been transferred from one medium to another for centuries. Even today, many of the ancient methods of design transfer are useful to the machine embroiderer. Thankfully, there are many options available because different fabrics and embroidery techniques require different transfer methods. It is easy, for example, to transfer a design to smooth, densely woven fabric by tracing it directly onto the fabric. You will need to use a straight stitch, however, when transferring a design onto fabric with a nap or high texture. The following is a brief description of the most commonly used methods of design transfer in machine embroidery.

DIRECT TRACING

Retrace the outline of the design in bold black ink on the original pattern so that it can be seen easily through fabric. Then secure the design to a light table or window with masking tape and attach the fabric on top of it with straight pins. The light will shine through the fabric, showing the lines of the design. Trace the design onto the fabric with chalk, a lead pencil, or water- or air-removable pen. This method is most successful with transparent and semi-transparent fabrics.

CUT PAPER METHOD

Cut away the paper around the design. Then pin or tape the centered design to hooped fabric. Machine straight stitch close to the cut edge, but not through the paper (Fig. 4.1). Remove the paper and the design is ready to embroider.

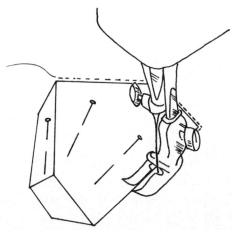

4.1 To transfer a pattern using the cut paper method, pin or tape the design to hooped fabric and machine straight stitch around the paper.

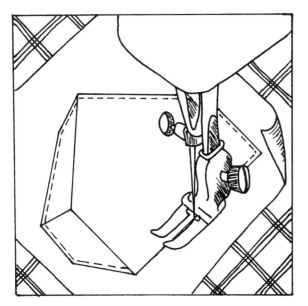

4.2 To transfer a pattern using the tissue paper method, trace the design onto tissue paper, attach the tissue paper to the fabric, and use the darning foot to sew the paper to the fabric.

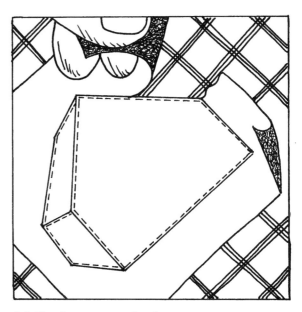

4.3 Gently tear away the tissue paper.

TISSUE PAPER OR TYPING PAPER TRACING

This is an easy method of transfer and one I use frequently. Trace your design onto typing paper or tissue paper and then attach the paper to the fabric to be embroidered. Be sure to pin the design firmly in place, whether the fabric is hooped or not. Pinning is also important if the design is larger than the hoop. Otherwise, the paper will move, thus altering the design during tracing. Attach the darning foot to the machine and lower the feed dogs. Bring up the bobbin thread to the surface through the fabric and paper. Use a high contrast thread color to sew a straight stitch on the design line through the paper and the fabric (Fig. 4.2). When you tear away the paper from the stitching, you will see that the design has been transferred (Fig. 4.3). Because it is difficult to remove paper from between two closely stitched lines, it is a good idea to simplify the design and use long machine stitches. The advantage to the tissue paper should now be obvious—it is easier to tear away.

With this method of transfer you may choose to transfer only the main lines of a design, then tear away the paper and use artistic license to complete it. You also have the option, if the design is symmetrical or if the reverse of the design would not ruin the flow, of stitching the design to the wrong side of the fabric. When transferring the design to the back of the fabric, it is not as critical to remove all of the paper. If you want to transfer the design to the wrong side of the fabric, but want to avoid ending up with the reverse of the design, simply use the light table or window to retrace the design onto the back side of the pattern. Use this new pattern and the design will no longer be reversed on the right side of the fabric.

DRESSMAKER'S CARBON TRANSFERRING

Dressmaker's carbon, which is usually available in yellow, white, red, and navy blue, is easy to use on smooth fabric. Lay the fabric on a firm surface, center the pattern on the material, and pin the top of the paper in place. Lift the pattern and place the carbon under the pattern. (Do not pin the carbon in place because the carbon may leave a pin mark on the fabric.) Use a ballpoint pen that has run out of ink to trace the lines. A good substitute for dressmaker's carbon is carbon commonly used in office forms. This type of carbon may smudge or run if it is not set by heat. Before beginning to embellish the design, press the transferred design with a hot iron if the fabric will allow it.

PRICK AND POUNCE METHOD

The prick and pounce method is one of the oldest forms of design transfer and one of the most accurate. It is also a good method to use when the design needs to be repeated several times.

Trace the design to a piece of firm paper such as typing paper. Place the design over a folded towel on a firm surface. With an old size 110/18 sewing machine needle puncture the paper by hand, every ⅛" (Fig. 4.4). If the design is not too intricate, try making the pounce holes by using the straight stitch on the sewing machine. Make sure the feed dogs are up and use an open toe embroidery foot and an old 110/18 needle.

4.4 To transfer a pattern using the prick and pounce method, trace the design onto a piece of paper. Use an old needle to prick holes in the paper along the lines of the pattern. Attach the pattern to the fabric.

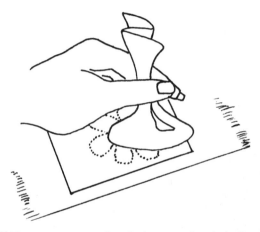

4.5 Prepare a pounce by placing powdered chalk, cornstarch, or talcum powder on a swatch of fabric. Gather the sides and corners together and rub the pouch over the design.

> ### Hint
> The design will transfer better if you use a piece of fine sandpaper to remove the bumps from the back of the punctured paper.

For dark and medium colored fabric prepare a pounce by putting one eighth of a cup of white chalk powder, corn starch, or talcum powder in the center of a 4" square of medium weight woven fabric. Bring the sides and corners to the center and secure with a rubber band. If the embroidery fabric is white or pastel use charcoal powder or cinnamon in the pounce.

To transfer the design, lay the fabric to be embroidered right side up, on a firm surface. Pin the prepared design face up in the correct position, and rub the pounce pouch over the design (Fig. 4.5). Check to see that the pounce is going through the holes by lifting a corner of the design. Remove the pattern if the design has been successfully transferred. The pattern is now outlined by little dots of the pounce. Carefully bring the fabric

to the machine and straight stitch (either free motion or with the presser foot, depending on the intricacy of the design) the pounce lines. Often I can get away with omitting the sewing step and simply proceeding with the embroidery by being careful not to disturb the pounce. If, like me, you sometimes prefer not to straight stitch the design after you have pounced it, you may use a water- or air-removable marker or chalk to trace the lines.

TRANSFER PAINT, CRAYONS, AND PENCILS

Iron-on transfers are made with transfer paint or a transfer pencil. Transfer paint is not readily available, but it is wonderful to use. The paint comes in six colors: red, blue, yellow, violet, green, and black. Use a brush, sponge, or spray to paint the design on regular typing paper. When the paint is dry, lay the paper painted side down on the right side of the fabric and press with a very hot, dry iron. Use a transfer pencil in the same way. These designs wash well if the fabric is at least 60% synthetic. See the Source List at the back of the book.

Transfer crayons called Crayola Fabric Colors are available in eight colors and work well when using light to medium color synthetic fabric. Draw the design on white paper with the crayons. Remember to brush the excess specks of crayon away. Place the design face down on the fabric and apply steady pressure—not an ironing motion—with a hot iron (cotton setting) until the design becomes slightly visible through the back of the paper. Remove the paper carefully. Do not bleach or put in a clothes dryer.

Both transfer paint and crayon patterns can be used several times, but the transfer will fade a little each time. Remember, with this method of transfer the design is reversed since the painted/drawn design is face down.

DRAWING THE DESIGN DIRECTLY TO FABRIC

You can do it. Practice on paper first and then use a water- or air-removable pen or fabric paint and a brush or pen to draw the design directly to fabric.

ENLARGING AND REDUCING DESIGNS

The easiest and fastest way to change the size of a design is to use a copy machine. But some of us live out in the boonies or near small towns that do not offer this service. In that case the following method is an easy solution. You will need paper, a sharp pencil, and a ruler. Trace the design onto paper and enclose the design in a

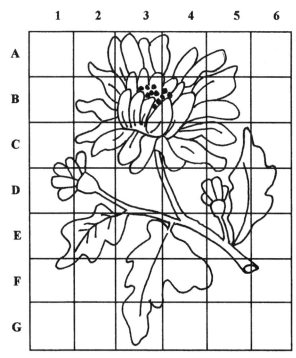

4.6 When you don't have access to a copy machine, you can change the size of a pattern by using the grid method.

box. Draw a grid over the design making each square equal (Fig. 4.6). On a second sheet of paper, draw a second box the new design size. In the second box draw a grid with the same number of equidistant squares as the original box. Alphabetize the squares down the side and number the squares across the top. Use a pencil to copy what you see in each square of the first grid into each corresponding square in the second grid.

TO HOOP OR NOT TO HOOP

No hoop is needed in machine embroidery when a presser foot is used and the feed dogs are in the up position. However, a hoop is a must in free motion embroidery to ensure that the fabric is held drum tight, allowing it to lay flat on the bed of the sewing machine.

Straight Stitch Exercise turned into an attractive placemat.

Bundle Belt.

Four Way Zigzag Make-up Bag.

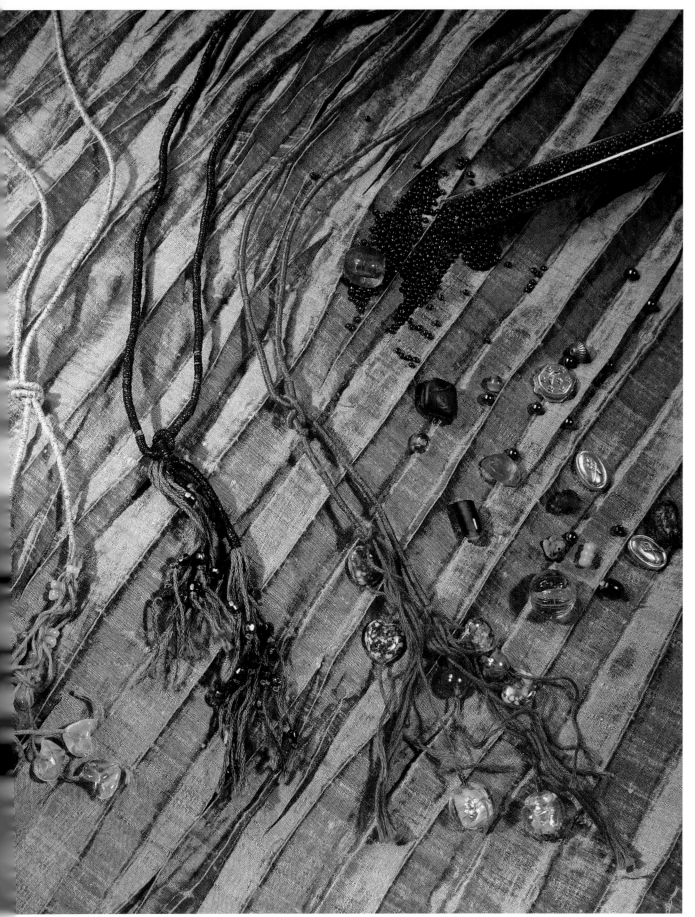

Necklace Cords.

Jacket Deluxe!

Burma Vest.

Top left: Printed fabric embellished with pre-programmed patterns; top right: programmed stitches over heavy threads; middle: fabric embellished with multi-color thread; bottom: solid fabric with pre-programmed stitches.

Patchwork Pin Cushion.

Two Spectacular Purses.

Upper left: Double/Twin Needle Bookmark; lower left: Zig and Zag Bargello Coin Purse; lower right: Embroidered Checkbook Cover.

Maribella in All Her Glory.

Pillow Puffing and Glads in Fill-in Stitch.

WHY HOOPS ARE IMPORTANT IN FREE MOTION MACHINE EMBROIDERY

Without a hoop or presser foot the fabric tends to follow the needle to its highest position. This is called flagging. Because flagging disturbs the path of the needle thread to the bobbin, the needle thread fails to snatch the bobbin thread from the hook and a skipped stitch occurs. So even though the sewing machine goes through the motion of forming a stitch, none is actually formed. Instead of being stitched into the fabric, the thread of a skipped stitch merely rests on top of the fabric between two completed stitches. These running threads, as skipped stitches are frequently called, are easily caught on a rough surface and break, causing stitches to come apart.

In addition to causing skipped stitches, unhooped fabric also increases wear on the thread during the sewing process, which causes thread breakage. Unhooped fabric is also prone to puckering. While puckering is not usually a problem when embroidering with a straight stitch, it is often a problem when using a zigzag stitch. This is because the tension on the thread as it moves from side to side causes the thread to pull on the fabric.

TYPES OF HOOPS

Embroidery hoops are made for different purposes. There are hoops for quilting, for hooking rugs, for hand embroidery, and for machine embroidery, to name a few. Since each type of hoop has a unique purpose, each is constructed a bit differently.

CHOOSING A GOOD HOOP

Machine embroidery hoops are constructed of wood with a metal screw that allows the hoop to be tightened and loosened. These wooden hoops made especially for machine embroidery are not as wide as hand embroidery hoops. Usually the wood is about a ¼" deep. The wood should be smooth and the edges beveled.

Some machine embroidery hoops have a shal-low half circle cut in both the inner and outer ring. This notch facilitates fitting the hoop under the needle. You may want to have someone cut a notch in your hoop as described if you have difficulty getting the hoop between the needle and the bed of the sewing machine.

The shape of the hoop is important since it affects the tension on the fabric. A round hoop holds the most consistent tension in all directions. Oval hoops maintain more tension lengthwise than widthwise. Square hoops maintain more tension diagonally.

You notice that so far I have spoken only of wooden hoops. That is because I speak reluctantly about metal and plastic hoops for machine embroidery. The better plastic hoops are those having a metal inner ring that fits into a groove in the outer plastic portion of the hoop; it is squeezed to release the fabric. This type of hoop should only be used on light weight fabric when it does not have to be moved, causing the embroidered area to be within the groove of the hoop. Dense embroidery or heavy fabric tend to cause the plastic hoop to pop open. Additionally, it is very difficult to have a taut surface upon which to work when the fabric is too heavy to fit comfortably in the groove of the hoop.

> ### Hint
>
> If you own a plastic hoop with a metal inner ring that does not pull the fabric tight, it is possible to increase the tension on the fabric in the hoop by removing the metal ring and stretching the two handles apart. Be careful when reinserting the metal ring back into the hoop as it now has lots of spring and may fly open if not secure in the outer ring.
>
> When using a hoop with an outer plastic ring and an inner metal ring, the squeeze handle may obstruct the movement of the hoop. Try to place the handle opposite the area you are embroidering.

Metal hoops have a built-in spring on the outside of the outer ring that stretches when the fabric is put in the hoop. There is no way to tighten the hoop once the fabric is hooped. The tightness you have is what you get. This type of hoop is not effective for machine embroidery.

When you buy a machine embroidery hoop, buy the best you can afford. Examine the hoop as you ponder purchasing it. Put the rings inside each other and screw the knob until it holds the inner ring firmly in place. Hold it up to the light; if you see no light between the rings you have found a good hoop.

HOOP SIZE

Hoop size is another consideration. A 6" hoop is essential for smaller projects. It is also the easiest to handle as you begin machine embroidery. As you continue learning machine embroidery you will want to add to your equipment an 8" hoop for moderately sized projects. The 8" hoop allows more stitching before you need to move the hoop to the next area to be embroidered. I also have a 12" hoop that I use when the embroidery is dense and massive. I find on those occasions that the fewer times I move the hoop the less possibility there is of puckers and skipped stitches. At the same time the hooped fabric lays more smoothly on the sewing machine bed.

WRAPPING THE INNER HOOP

Wrapping the inner ring of the hoop has its pros and cons. Inner hoops are wrapped to help give a tighter grip on the fabric as it is held in place by the inner and outer hoops. People also wrap inner rings to avoid the possibility of marring or damaging the fabric and when embroidering a very light weight fabric.

Most teachers recommend wrapping the inner hoop. I don't think that should be a cardinal rule and I'll tell you why. First of all, rarely will wrapping be necessary if you purchase a hoop of good quality. Second, the fabric used to wrap the inner ring is easily soiled and may soil the fabric in the hoop. The biggest reason, however, for an unwrapped hoop is that extreme care must be taken to wrap smoothly. If the fabric is wrapped in such a way that there are several layers in one spot and only one layer in another, you have negated the reason for wrapping the hoop in the first place. Additionally, when the inner hoop is wrapped it is much more difficult to pull the fabric taut before giving the screw a final turn. This is often necessary on an 8" hoop and larger.

If you choose to wrap a hoop here is how it is done. Wrap the ring that does not have the screw with cotton twill tape, or seam binding ½" wide. (Recently, someone told me that an old nylon stocking cut in strips and wrapped around the inner hoop works well.) Wrap smoothly, overlapping each wrap by about ¼". End the wrap on the inside of the hoop by hand stitching it in place.

Some people have found success gluing ¼" velvet ribbon on the outside edge of the inner ring. Allow the glue to dry completely before using the hoop. I have also heard that sandpaper may be used to rough up both the inside edge of the outer ring and the outer ring of the inner hoop. I do not recommend this practice, however, because the rough surface of the hoop may cause irreparable damage to the fabric.

HOOPING HEAVY FABRICS

A deeper hoop helps to hold bulky or slick fabric. These hoops are called embroidery hoops and are ½" to 1" deep and vary in quality. Because these hoops are so thick, the needle must be removed each time the hoop is removed from the bed of the sewing machine.

HOOPING FABRIC

Now that we understand why fabric needs to be taut for machine embroidery, let's hoop some fabric. Practice a couple of times, and you should have this important element down pat.

It is impossible to tightly hoop your fabric while holding it in front of you as you are sitting down. Give yourself a chance to stretch, then stand up and adjust the screw so that it is loosened by two turns. Lay the outer ring on the

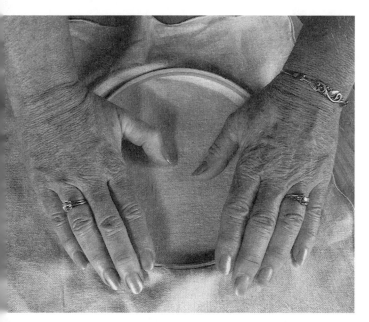

4.7 To tightly hoop your fabric, place your fabric right side up on top of the outer embroidery ring, then lay the inner ring on top. With the fingertips of both hands, push the far sides of the inner ring down into the outer ring.

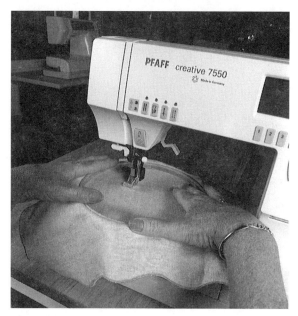

4.8 Make sure the embroidery hoop and fabric lay flat on the bed of the sewing machine.

table. Place the fabric right side up, with the portion to be embroidered centered over the outer ring on the table. Lay the inner ring on top. With the fingertips of both hands, push the far side of the inner ring down into the outer ring. Remove one hand and straighten the fabric so that the grain is true. Put that hand back in position and push the inner ring down the rest of the way. Using the palms of both hands, go around the entire circumference of the hoop (Fig. 4.7). Please note that you are putting the fabric in the hoop in the opposite manner of hand embroidery.

I cannot emphasize enough how important it is to make sure the vertical and horizontal (warp and weft) threads of the fabric are straight in the hoop. If a fabric with a crooked grain is embroidered on, the embroidery will not lay flat when it is released from the hoop. The stitching will have permanently distorted the fabric. Be careful not to stretch knit fabric while hooping because permanent distortion will occur in these fabrics as well. When embroidering on stretch fabric or fabric that is easily marred by the hoop, place a piece of tissue paper over the fabric and then

hoop it all in place. Before beginning to embroider tear the tissue paper away within the circumference of the hoop.

The fabric should be drum tight and pucker free in the hoop. If not, remove it from the hoop and try again, adjusting the screw as needed. Rarely am I able to achieve the correct level of tautness on the first try. It takes several turns of the screw and it depends on the thickness of the fabric.

When machine embroidering using an embroidery hoop it is important that the hoop be able to lay flat on the bed of the sewing machine. To facilitate this your sewing machine should have a flat bed (Fig. 4.8). If your machine is a free-arm, always attach the removable sewing table when embroidering with a hoop. If the machine bed is slanted you will need to hold on to the hoop tightly and keep it level while moving it!

If you are unable to finish all of the embroidery within the hooped area in one sitting, do not be tempted to leave the hoop on the fabric until the next time you stitch. If you do, you may find that the fabric has a permanent ring the size and shape of the hoop.

HOW TO USE STABILIZERS

The stabilizer is usually placed under the fabric. Then the stitching is done through the fabric and the stabilizer. If the stitching is dense or if a firm finished fabric is desired the stabilizer may be left in place. Otherwise it is torn away around the edge of the embroidery after the stitching is finished.

The type and amount of stabilizer needed is different for each fabric and embroidery design. Weight is a significant factor. The stabilizer should be slightly lighter than the fabric. If the stabilizer is too heavy it will weigh down the fabric and distort its shape and drapability. The density of the embroidery is also a factor. Dense embroidery requires a firm stabilizer.

I will suggest the best stabilizer to use with each project in this book. In general, a tear away stabilizer is useful when there is no need for added stiffness in the finished project. An iron-on tear away stabilizer is useful when a hoop cannot be used.

Cold water stabilizer is the stabilizer of choice when no added stiffness or added fiber can remain after the embroidery is finished. Hot water stabilizer is used when no added stiffness can be tolerated in a very dense embroidery. (Often this type of embroidery is made entirely of thread after the stabilizer is melted away.)

Liquid stabilizers are used when a fabric can tolerate a liquid applied to it and when no hoop can be used.

Hoops used in combination with a stabilizer are the surest way to prevent fabric and embroidery distortion. It is common to put the stabilized fabric into a hoop. I must admit that often I only hoop the fabric. (Always be careful that the grain of the fabric is straight.) Then I simply lay a tear away stabilizer under the hoop and stitch through all the layers. Often it is necessary to use two or three layers of stabilizer to produce a firm enough surface to finish with a fine embroidery.

Another method of stabilization is especially useful when the embroidery will be on a small piece of fabric that is difficult to hoop. Hoop the stabilizer and then pin the fabric tautly to the stabilizer.

Felt and quilt batting make other interesting stabilizers. When either is used the stitches sink into the fabric and have a quilted, cushioned appearance.

The use of a stabilizer frequently changes the stitch appearance if the needle thread tension is not adjusted to accommodate it. Usually the needle thread tension needs to be decreased a small amount.

There are many stabilizers on the market. Here is a brief overview of the current types of stabilizers along with relevant brand names:

- Iron-on interfacing
  HeatnBond Lite, Tuf-Fuse, Soft Shape Iron On Interfacing

- Tear away (non-woven)
  Easy Stitch, No-Whiskers, Tear Easy

- Cold water stabilizer (like translucent plastic)
  Avalon, Solvy, Aqua Solve, RinsAway

- Hot water stabilizer (like woven organdy)
  Melt-A-Way

- Liquid stabilizer/paint or spray-on stabilizer
  Perfect Sew, Helmar Lite Fabric Stiffener

- Heat removable stabilizer (heavy woven fabric)
  Vanish-a-Way

- Iron on (attaching one fabric to another)
  Wonder Under, Finefuse, Stitch Witchery

- Any woven transparent fabric (organdy)

- Paper (copy, tissue, or newspaper)

- Starch, liquid or spray

- Aerosol spray stabilizer

THE TWO METHODS OF MACHINE EMBROIDERY

There are two methods of doing machine embroidery. The first is to use the sewing machine in the usual way, with the presser foot in place and the feed dogs up, thus automatically moving the material away from you with each stitch the machine makes.

The second method of machine embroidery is called free motion and is by far the more exciting. In free motion embroidery, the regular presser foot is removed; some people attach a darning foot, while others embroider without any attachment. In either case, the feed dogs are lowered or covered, which means that the embroiderer has to move the fabric by hand. Any sewing machine can do this method of embroidery, although some machines do it easier than others.

MACHINE EMBROIDERY WITH PRE-PROGRAMMED STITCHES

If you have a basic machine that does a straight and zigzag stitch and a few utility stitches all is not lost. Many interesting patterns can be created using these stitches. See Chapters Five and Six for inventive projects using the straight stitch and the zigzag stitch. But if you have built-in or pre-programmed stitches, take a few moments to complete the following exercise. It will help increase your familiarity with your machine and its pre-programmed stitches.

1. Insert a new 90/14 needle.

2. Thread needle with machine embroidery thread.

3. Fill bobbin with machine embroidery bobbin thread. Use white or black depending on the color of fabric.

4. Decrease top tension by one number. This allows the top thread to be pulled to the back of the fabric and forces the needle thread to lay smoothly on the surface of the fabric. Test the tension on a scrap of fabric that you will be using in the embroidery. Choose a medium weight solid color fabric.

5. Stabilize the fabric with an iron-on tear away stabilizer of medium weight.

6. Draw a vertical line 1" from the edge as a guide for the first row of stitching.

7. Choose any stitch and sew along the drawn line. Begin stitching slowly so that you are able to guide the fabric accurately. Iron the embroidery frequently to decrease the possibility of puckers.

8. Elongate the same stitch by increasing the stitch length. Then try increasing and decreasing the stitch width, sewing a row of each a presser foot apart. Note how this changes the pattern. On some model machines the density of the thread remains the same when the length is changed. On older machines the density decreases as the stitch is elongated.

9. Choose a stitch that is asymmetrical. Stitch one row and then try the mirror image feature, which is sometimes called the turn over memory key. This is a fun way to add variety. You will notice that the pattern is stitched so that the right and left are reversed.

10. Next engage the pattern start feature. Notice that the way the pattern is pictured on the display or door of the machine is how it looks when it is stitched. The pattern starts in the upper left each time. This is a useful feature if the thread breaks and you need a continuous row. You can insert the needle at the beginning of the last pattern (even if that is not where the thread broke) and proceed from that point.

11. The single pattern feature allows you to stitch one complete pattern, after which the machine will automatically stop. This is a wonderful feature when you want to stitch a single flower, for example. Go ahead, give it a try.

12. Consult your sewing machine manual to learn to program the machine to stitch one complete pattern followed by a completely different pattern. For variety's sake, pick patterns you haven't tried yet in this exercise. Most machines today will allow you to program between thirty and eighty-five patterns to follow one another. If more patterns are needed continue in the next memory.

13. Many machines allow a choice of needle positions from right to left. This feature often makes it easier to stitch on the seam edge, to top stitch, or quilt. Try a 4mm wide satin stitch, stitching 1" then changing the needle position and repeating.

Add this exercise to your collection of plastic pages.

FREE MOTION EMBROIDERY

Now try the second type of machine embroidery, free motion embroidery, which is often called darning in sewing machine manuals. Free motion embroidery allows the embroiderer to move the fabric in any direction, horizontally and vertically. The speed at which the embroiderer moves the fabric and the speed of the machine, regulated by the foot pedal, allow the embroiderer an infinite variety of stitch length, width, and density.

In free motion embroidery the feed dogs are lowered (usually by a button or lever). Some machines provide a plastic or metal cover that is easily inserted over the dogs. If your machine does not allow for the lowering of the feed dogs or supply a cover, cover the feed dogs with tape that can be removed easily. Remember to make a small hole in the tape for the bobbin thread. When using tape to cover the feed dogs, set the stitch length control at zero. This will decrease the motion of the feed dogs to the least amount possible.

As an exercise in preparation for free motion embroidery please copy the four patterns found at the end of this chapter (p. 50).

1. Begin the exercise by removing all thread from the sewing machine. Insert an old needle, use a regular presser foot and the feed dogs. Use a straight stitch on the straight lines of the upper right pattern. Sew over the lines as fast as possible without straying from the line. Stitch six lines.

2. Go on to the rectangle. Begin on the outside edge and complete one half of the rectangle with a straight stitch, still using the presser foot and feed dogs.

3. Next, stitch the circle by beginning on the outside edge. Stitch half the circle.

4. Last, stitch a few inches of the squiggles.

Now that you have completed the first half of the exercise in regular machine embroidery mode, prepare your sewing machine for free motion embroidery.

1. Remove the presser foot and ankle.

2. Lower feed dogs by following the instructions in your sewing machine manual. There are three possible ways:
    a) Push a lever or turn a knob that automatically lowers the dogs.
    b) Cover the feed dogs with the plastic cover provided with the machine.
    c) Cover the feed dogs with tape. Make a hole in the tape for the bobbin thread to pass through and large enough for the machine to zigzag. Set the stitch length at zero to decrease the motion of the feed dogs to the least amount possible.

3. Prepare the fabric for embroidery by
    a) stabilizing the fabric,
    b) putting the fabric in a machine embroidery hoop (see "To Hoop or Not to Hoop" earlier in this chapter),
    c) or both of the above.

4. Decrease the top tension by one number. Consult your manual since every machine is different. Most commonly there is a dial on the top left of the machine. Usually 4–5 is a balanced stitch.

5. Place hooped fabric under the needle flat on the bed of the sewing machine.

6. LOWER THE PRESSER BAR LEVER. As you proceed you will understand why I have written this in capital letters. When the presser foot is removed it is very easy to forget to lower the lever. Lowering the presser foot lever engages the top tension. Some machines are more forgiving than others. Some will form a stitch, although poorly, when the lever is up. Most, however, will sound terrible and immediately cause a snarl on the underside of the fabric. If this happens to you, do not continue stitching in the hope that it will correct itself. It will only get worse. If you persist the snarl will be so bad that you will need to remove the cover plate to cut out the knotted thread. At the first odd sound, stop the sewing machine and check the presser foot lever. Rethread the sewing machine and then try again, remembering to lower the presser bar.

7. Bring the bobbin thread to the surface by taking a single stitch and holding on to the needle thread. By putting tension on the needle thread, the bobbin thread is forced through the needle hole to the surface of the fabric. If the machine is a current model take a single stitch using the foot pedal. If not, take one stitch manually by turning the hand wheel towards you. Bringing the bobbin thread to the surface removes the possibility of a knotted mess on the underside of the fabric.

8. Take a few straight stitches. This anchors both bobbin and needle threads. Cut the thread ends away as close as possible to the fabric and continue stitching.

Now you are ready to finish the second half of the exercise. Repeat steps one through four in the free motion mode by beginning where you left off before. REMEMBER TO LOWER THE PRESSER BAR LEVER. While you are proceeding you will begin to notice a new freedom. As you approach a corner in the rectangle, for example, you no longer have to stop and change stitching direction. Instead, you simply change the direction in which you move the paper.

As you begin stitching the squiggles the benefit of free motion embroidery will become immediately apparent. Now the paper can be moved in any direction so that the needle can follow the line. For practice finish embroidering all of the patterns in this exercise. Add this exercise to your collection of plastic pages.

Pre-programmed embroidery and free motion embroidery are the two basic techniques of machine embroidery. Now that you have practiced both methods you are ready to create the projects in the remainder of the book. You will be amazed at how easy it is to create the projects in Chapter Five, each of which is embroidered entirely in straight stitch.

Pattern 4a

Part Two

Stitches

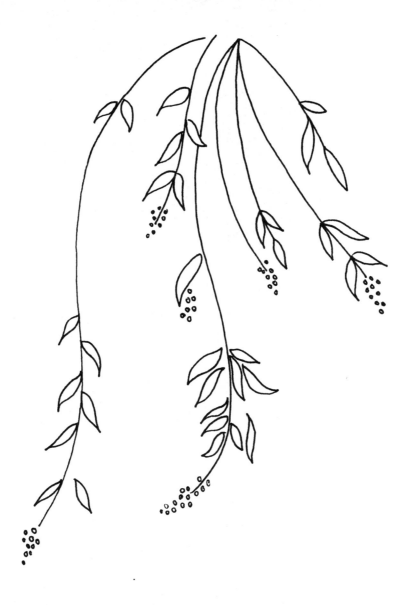

5 *Chapter Five*

Simply Straight Stitch

Embroidery You Can Do on Any Sewing Machine

> *All glory comes from daring to begin.*
> —Eugene F. Ware

Everything the sewing machine does mimics what hands can do, but the sewing machine does it faster. The straight stitch of the machine echoes the double running stitch of hand work, in which both the front and the back of the fabric are covered by a thread that forms a line.

A good-looking, durable straight stitch on the sewing machine is flat, does not move or have loops, and is pucker free. The needle and bobbin threads meet and lock in the center between the two fabric layers. This holds them together tightly.

The straight stitch as a tool for machine embroidery is one of the most exciting design elements the machine embroiderer has. This means that everyone who owns even the oldest of the old sewing machines can use her machine as a tool to create embroidery.

In this chapter, through exercises and specific projects, I will show you how the straight stitch can be used in embroidery to create any mood, in any technique. Be sure to do the exercises since they will help you learn techniques that you can then use to make projects of your own devising as well as the projects included in this book.

Beginners especially will love these projects as they require only the straight stitch and a presser foot.

Let's begin.

Card Frenzy

 YOUR FRIENDS WILL LOVE RECEIVING THESE CHARMING CARDS MADE FROM THREADS AND SMALL SCRAPS OF FABRIC LEFT OVER FROM YOUR LAST SEWING PROJECT.

5.1 Card Frenzy.

Supplies

- Cards with a cut-out mat-like front with envelopes
- ¼ yard of tulle in a color to match or complement the scraps cut to the size of the closed card
- One spool of metallic 40 wt machine embroidery thread any color
- One spool of machine embroidery bobbin thread
- Batting or Thermolan the size of the inside of the card
- Medium weight fabric the size of the inside of the card
- Transparent tape
- 90/14 needle
- Embroidery presser foot
- Thread snips, all so-called orts, and small scraps of fabric

HOW TO

1. Lay batting on a flat surface.

2. Lay one layer of fabric over batting.

3. Make color and texture choices from the scraps. Be sure to use thread scraps as well as fabric scraps. Lay the scraps over the layer of fabric in a pleasing design (Fig. 5.2). Try to balance color and texture by repeating the placement of the same color scraps in three places in the design. Keep in mind that your design needs a focal point, a place the eye naturally returns to within the

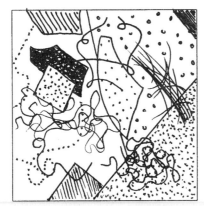

5.2 Lay snips of thread and scraps of fabric over ¼ yard of tulle.

design. Focal points are best when placed off center. Center of interest is another name for a focal point. Think about creating visual interest as you determine the placement of the scraps.

4. When the design is complete place a single layer of tulle over all and pin in place.

5. Thread a 90/14 needle with the metallic thread and the bobbin with the bobbin thread.

6. Use a satin stitch or embroidery presser foot on the machine.

7. Set the sewing machine to straight stitch 2.5mm in length.

8. Sew through all layers in random directions using forward and reverse stitching. The metallic thread in the needle will begin to stand out from the scraps and create its own design. Stop stitching frequently to look at the overall design. When the scraps have been secured and the design is pleasing it is time to stop stitching!

9. To finish, cut the embroidery to fit in the card and use transparent tape to hold in place and hold the card closed.

FREE MOTION EMBROIDERY WITH STRAIGHT STITCH

The following projects all are stitched in the free motion embroidery mode. The directions instruct you to attach a darning foot. You may, however, use an embroidery spring or spring needle. If you're feeling confident, you may want to use the needle only. Many machine embroiderers remove all feet during machine embroidery in the free motion mode because it increases the visibility of the embroidered area. If you decide to embroider without a foot, be sure that your fabric is very tight in a machine embroidery hoop. You will need to use both index fingers on either side of the needle to press the fabric tight against the bed of the sewing machine as each stitch is being formed.

Be sure to keep your eyes on the needle at all times. If someone speaks to you and you need to look away, stop the machine, and then look up.

> ### Hint
> I find that if I avoid coffee, tea, and chocolate for two to three hours before I begin to do free motion embroidery in straight stitch that my rows of stitches are much less jagged. All of those great tasting things act as stimulants and tend to make fine motor skills unsteady.

MANIPULATING THE STRAIGHT STITCH SHAPE AND FORM TO CREATE DESIGNS

The basic element of design is a spot. In machine embroidery a spot is a single stitch. Several spots can form a line, a row of straight stitching. Lines—whether they are straight, curved, broken, or bent—when connected form a shape.

Some lines are thin, some thick, others light or dark. Add to this the dimensions of overlapping lines and a whole array of possible shapes can be created. Peg Laflam's vest in the black-and-white photo is a good example of how the design line in the marbled fabric is mimicked by the straight stitch embroidery (Fig. 5.3).

As we work with line in all its variations, it portrays meaning. For example, a dark, bold line may suggest distance, while a narrow, fine line may give a sense of nearness and movement.

HOW TO MAKE CONSISTENT FREE MOTION EMBROIDERY STITCHES

- Practice, practice, practice!

- If possible, set the speed of the sewing machine to half speed.

- Most beginners need to decrease the speed of the sewing machine and increase the speed of the hoop. If the sewing machine is stitching

fast and the hoop is barely moving the stitches will be sewn almost in place. When several stitches are taken in the same place the thread wears and then breaks. The technique is much like learning to rub your tummy and pat your head. But if you can't do that, however, don't worry. I can't rub my tummy and pat my head at the same time, but I can do free machine embroidery. And you can too.

- For better control, hold on to the hoop with both hands.

- Keep the fabric taut in the hoop so that it sounds like a drum when tapped. That way, there will be minimal thread wear as the needle goes in and out of the fabric. Additionally, a taut hoop is safer because it eliminates the need to have one's fingers right up close to the needle.

- Read Chapter Eight: When Things Go Wrong.

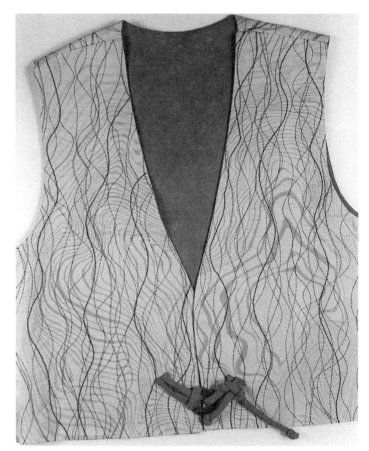

5.3 A vest made by Peg Laflam shows how easy it is to mimic marbled fabric using nothing more than the straight stitch.

Straight Stitch Exercise
(see color section)

 DO YOU DOODLE WHEN YOU TALK ON THE PHONE? If so, you'll appreciate this colorful exercise, which lets you doodle to your heart's content. What's more, once you have the machine embroidery doodling technique down pat, you'll be able to make all kinds of useful and attractive household items. Try this technique with table runners, placemats, napkins, pillows, and quilts.

Before you begin, practice the following techniques on paper. Fold an 8½" x 11" piece of paper into thirty-two 1½" x 2" rectangles. With a number two pencil, draw vertical, horizontal, diagonal left to right, and diagonal right to left lines in the first four boxes, then begin your own creative doodling in the boxes that remain. In

5.4 For this straight stitch exercise, divide a piece of paper into thirty-two rectangles. Draw doodles and images in each of the rectangles, then re-create these images on fabric by using your sewing machine needle as though it were a pencil.

Fig. 5.4 there are curved, bent, broken, and straight lines to inspire you.

In addition to creating random shapes, you can reproduce designs you see around you. Look for design ideas in your environment, including fabric patterns and dish designs, scenic views and flower petals, jewelry and even bubbles in a bathtub (see Fig. 5.4). You can do it. In class, when the students are finished, I have them turn the page over and complete the second set of thirty-two rectangles. The practice gives them lots of great ideas to work with.

Now transfer this same exercise to your sewing machine.

Supplies

- Medium weight, tightly woven 10½" x 12" fabric (black is elegant and usually enhances machine embroidery thread colors)
- Several spools of 40 wt machine embroidery rayon and/or metallic thread
- 90/14 needle
- 70 wt polyester bobbin thread in the bobbin
- Darning presser foot
- 8" machine embroidery hoop
- Chalk and ruler

HOW TO

Review "Free Motion Embroidery" in Chapter Four.

1. Divide the fabric into thirty-two 1½" x 2" rectangles with chalk and ruler. Using the straight stitch, stitch over the lines with 40 wt rayon machine embroidery thread.

2. Lower the feed dogs.

3. Decrease the needle tension by one number.

4. Attach the darning foot.

5. Put the fabric in the machine embroidery hoop.

Hint

Even though you are stitching in the free motion embroidery mode, you do not need to use a stabilizer because a hoop is holding the fabric taut and the straight stitch is being used exclusively.

6. Bring the bobbin thread to the surface.

7. Begin entering each of the line drawings in a different box. Try to duplicate each of the thirty-two line drawings you drew on paper by using your sewing machine needle as if it were your pencil.

8. Keep stitching in all directions until you are pleased with the design. You may need to stitch over stitching already done.

Hint

For greater variety, keep the following points in mind.
- Change direction and bend the stitching line by moving the fabric in a different direction.
- Overlap some stitches.
- Stitch several lines right next to each other.
- Variety may be added by changing the needle thread color every now and then.
- Complete all of the designs you have drawn in the rectangles on the fabric.
- For variety, change the needle thread to 40 wt metallic.

As you can see, lines are an interesting basic element of design, so why not start keeping a record of the stitch exercises? Place the line drawing and sewing sample back to back in clear plastic insert pages in a notebook for future reference.

Free Motion Embroidery on Pre-printed Fabric

 EMBROIDERING ON PRE-PRINTED FABRIC GIVES YOU THE FREEDOM TO CREATE BEAUTIFUL, EMBELL-ISHED PIECES WITHOUT HAVING TO TRANSFER A PATTERN. Even better, if you have a fabric pattern you like in colors you dislike, you can stitch over the pattern in colors of your own choosing: the original colors will not show through. The number of colors you need depends on the scope and size of the pre-printed pattern, but I suggest using six colors the first time around. I like to use fabric showing flowers and animals, although repeat geometric patterns work well too. The first time you try this technique, use a piece of fabric that is approximately 8" x 10" as it will be easier to manipulate when using a hoop.

5.5 A sampler made by machine embroidering over pre-printed fabric.

Supplies

- Pre-printed picture on medium weight fabric
- Six different colors of cotton or rayon 40 wt machine embroidery thread
- White machine embroidery bobbin thread
- 6" wooden machine embroidery hoop
- 9/14 universal or machine embroidery needle
- Darning foot or spring embroidery foot
- Iron-on stabilizer the size of the fabric (see Source List at back of book)

HOW TO

Reread "Free Motion Embroidery" in Chapter Four.

1. Decrease the needle tension by one number.

2. Lower or cover the feed dogs.

3. Insert a new 90/14 needle, remove presser foot, and attach darning foot or spring needle or embroidery spring.

4. Pick a starting point (I began with the leaves in the sample) and thread the bobbin and needle with the appropriate colors of machine embroidery thread.

5. Iron stabilizer to back of fabric.

6. Hoop stabilized fabric (see Chapter Four for hooping instructions). Be sure there is a ½" of fabric between the pattern and the inner edge of the hoop. This will ensure that the needle does not run into the hoop while you are stitching.

7. Place hoop under needle. Use the sewing table that comes with free-arm machines as this will help to balance the hoop during embroidery.

8. Lower the presser foot lever.

9. Take a single stitch and pull the bobbin thread to the surface (Fig. 5.6).

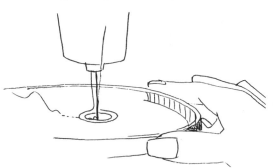

5.6 Take a single stitch and pull the bobbin thread to the surface.

Hint

For variety, try the following ideas.

- Put a layer of batting between the fabric and the stabilizer. This will give the embroidery a quilted look.
- Rayon embroidery thread has a wonderful sheen. To capitalize on this feature, stitch with longer stitches by running the machine at a moderate speed and moving the hoop faster.
- Fill in some petals completely and leave others mostly bare by outlining them and then stitching only two or three radiating lines from the base of each petal.
- Fill some areas in by stitching in radiating circles from the center out.
- Try metallic thread for the entire embroidery. Be sure to use a 100/16 needle.
- Sign your name by writing it in an inconspicuous place with a air-removable pen. Stitch over it with a straight stitch.
- Combine rayon and metallic thread on one piece of embroidery.
- Using a floral print fabric, embroider two small motifs and then a larger motif. Frame the smaller motifs in two small frames and the larger motif in a larger frame. Two 5" x 7" frames and one 8" x 10" frame work well together.
- Use free motion embroidery to embellish the yoke of a print blouse you already own. Stitch only a few motifs, for example, on one shoulder.

10. Use the straight stitch of the machine like a pencil to outline the pattern. Next, fill in the design using rows of free motion straight stitches, changing color as desired. Move the hoop as needed, remembering to hoop the fabric so that it is taut in the hoop. It will help to iron the fabric, on the wrong side, each time the embroidery is removed from the hoop.

11. To finish, press and frame or make into a pillow. If your pattern is the right size, try adding it to a garment or add this exercise to a clear plastic page.

Developing your free motion embroidery skills can take a little time, and so I hope you will try this exercise several times. It's a great excuse to go to the fabric store!

Pillow Puffing
(see color section)

 THIS IS A FUN PROJECT THAT WILL GIVE YOU ADDED PRACTICE IN FOLLOWING THE LINES DURING FREE MOTION EMBROIDERY. The puffed appearance of the finished embroidery is produced with the use of batting and by the natural pulling of the fabric as it is embroidered without a hoop. You will note that the pillow form should be 14" x 14" while the finished inside pillow area is 16" x 16". The difference in size will make it easier to topstitch the flange after the pillow form is in the embroidered case. If the pillow form is too large you will have trouble topstitching the pillow closed. In addition, the flange may ripple rather than lay flat if the pillow is over-stuffed.

HOW TO

1. Prepare the sewing machine for free motion embroidery by attaching the darning foot, lowering the feed dogs, decreasing the needle tension by one number, and inserting a new 90/14 needle.

2. Thread the needle with 40 wt rayon thread and the bobbin with the bobbin thread.

3. Place the batting on the wrong side of the print fabric and pin the batting and the fabric together by placing the pins on the right side of the print fabric.

4. Place the pinned fabric under the needle and bring the bobbin thread to the surface. Set the sewing machine for straight stitch.

Supplies
- 14" X 14" pillow form (or purchase stuffing and make your own)
- *Pillow front:* All over print fabric 17" x 17"
- *Pillow back:* One piece of contrasting solid color fabric 20" x 20"
- *Pillow front border:* Two pieces 3" x 16" and two pieces 3" x 20"
- Rayon 40 wt thread in a very bright color to complement and highlight the all over print fabric
- Machine embroidery bobbin thread
- Darning or embroidery foot
- One 17" x 17" and one 20" x 20" piece of batting
- New 9/14 needle
- Construction thread to match fabric
- Zipper foot

5. Begin embroidering by outlining the motifs on the fabric. Run the sewing machine fast and move the fabric fast as well. Use your hands to keep the fabric as taut and close to the throat plate as possible. This takes a little practice. Keep in mind that no matter how taut the fabric, the stitches will still pull the fabric and cause a puffed look, which is just the look you want to achieve. (A hoop would avoid the puffs and keep the fabric smooth.) Continue outlining all of the motifs in this manner.

6. When finished, cut all threads close to the embroidery.

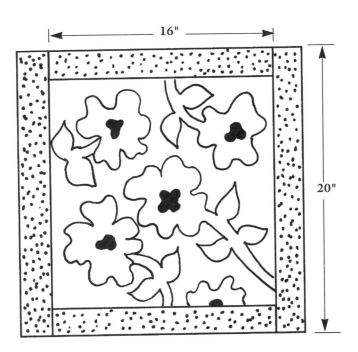

5.7 Sew the two 3" x 16" strips onto opposite ends of the finished Pillow Puffing embroidery, then sew the two 3" x 20" strips onto the two remaining ends.

FINISHING

1. Trim finished embroidery to 16" x 16".

2. Using a ½" seam allowance, sew the two 3" x 16" strips onto opposite ends of the finished embroidery. Press the seam flat away from the embroidery. Again using a ½" seam allowance, sew the two 3" x 20" strips on the two remaining ends, starting at the edge of the previous strip sewn (Fig. 5.7). Press seam.

3. Place the embroidery right side up over the 20" x 20" piece of batting. Then place the solid color fabric right side down on top of the embroidery. Pin the three layers together.

4. Using a ½" seam allowance, stitch three sides together. Using the same seam allowance, stitch the fourth side so that there is a 10" opening in the center. Press, clip corners, and turn right side out.

5. Pin all layers where strips join embroidery, except at opening.

6. Attach zipper foot and stitch in the ditch all around the pillow except at the opening. Stitching in the ditch means to straight stitch in the seam where the fabrics join. By stitching between the print fabric and the solid color fabric, a smaller inside pocket is formed, which will hold the pillow form centered in the pillow. Use the needle down feature to help turn the corners.

7. Insert the pillow form. Stitch in the ditch to close first seam. Slip stitch outer seam closed.

The Burma Vest
(see color section)

IF YOU ARE REALLY READY FOR A CHALLENGE, TRY CREATING THIS UNUSUAL VEST. YOU CAN EMBELL- ISH THE ENTIRE VEST USING ONLY THE STRAIGHT STITCH WITH A PRESSER FOOT. By using heavy thread in the needle combined with the frequent change of forward and reverse stitching, you will create a unique garment. Please keep in mind that all directions are given for vest (right and left) as the vest is being worn.

HOW TO

1. Pre-shrink all fabrics by washing them in the washer in warm water and detergent.

2. Decrease top (needle) tension by one number for all machine embroidery for this project.

3. Cut entire vest from lining fabric.

4. Cut the vest back out of stripe #1, with the stripes running vertically.

Supplies

• Lined vest pattern with a jewel neckline and abutting front edges (see color photo)

• Lining fabric for entire vest (a solid colored polished cotton will coordinate nicely with printed exterior vest fabric)

• A 1¹⁄₂" wide two-color stripe (to be referred to as stripe #1), enough for the entire vest plus ¹⁄₄ yard; I chose a 100% cotton Waverly drapery fabric (see Source List)

• A second 1¹⁄₂" wide two-color stripe (to be referred to as stripe #2) in a contrasting or comple- menting color; purchase half the amount called for on the pattern (in the sample, stripe #1 is pink and white, while stripe #2 is green and white)

• A print fabric to complement the two striped fabrics, ¹⁄₄ the amount required to make the vest (this print should have a discernible pattern, such as a medium size flower pattern 3"–4" in size)

• Four to eight spools of Burmilana thread by Madeira that coordinate with the chosen fabrics (if you don't have any Burmilana, try rayon 30 wt machine embroidery thread)

• One spool of white machine embroidery bobbin thread

• Enough light weight batting material to make the vest

• One package of 18/110 sewing machine needles for embroidery with Burmilana thread

• Two 90/14 needles for construction of the vest

• Construction thread in appropriate color to sew vest together (choose thread that matches the most dominant color in your fabrics)

• One spool of monofilament thread to attach the flower buttons

• Regular, embroidery, and walking presser feet

• Optional: a Perfect Pleater by Clotilde to help make ¹⁄₄" pleats (see Source List at back of book)

5. Cut right and left front pattern pieces from stripe #1, with the stripes running horizontally.

6. Cut batting for vest left and back.

7. For a size 12 pattern, cut a 22" wide by 12" long piece of stripe #2, with the stripes running vertically. For each pattern size larger or smaller add or subtract 2" to the width and length. This fabric will be tucked for the upper left front of the vest.

8. Cut 60" total of stripes #1 and #2 horizontally across the stripes. Vary the width of the stripe between ¾" and 1¼".

9. Cut one motif from the print fabric for the lower left front of the vest.

10. Cut two 9" x 1" strips of print fabric for fabric button.

11. Cut two 7" x 1⅔" strips from lining fabric for buttonhole loops.

12. Cut print fabric 30" long, the width of one side of upper right front pattern plus 1". This will be stitched and tucked and placed on the upper right front of the vest.

TOP LEFT FRONT VEST PANEL

(as you are wearing vest)

On stripe #2 that you created in step #7 in the previous section, sew vertical lines ⅛" apart as follows.

1. Decide what order the Burmilana colors will be sewn in and lay them on a table in that order. Alternate light and dark colors, for instance.

2. Using a 18/110 needle, thread the machine with the first color of Burmilana and wind the bobbin with machine embroidery bobbin thread.

3. Use a machine embroidery presser foot and dual feed dogs or an even feed walking foot if you have it.

4. Machine stitch length at 4mm long. Decrease needle tension by one number.

5. Using the first color Burmilana, sew one line of straight stitching in each of the light colored stripes. Remove this spool from the machine and place it at the end of your chosen spools. Then change to the second thread color and sew a second row of stitching ⅛" from first row. Repeat color sequence until the stripes chosen are filled (Fig. 5.8). Continue rows of stitching ⅛" apart using each color in the sequence you have selected. Remember to place the last used spool at the end of the sequence of spools and to next stitch with the first spool working left to right. Repeat until the lightest color striped area is covered with ⅛" apart rows of stitching.

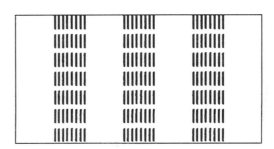

5.8 On the striped fabric, sew lines of straight stitching, one color thread after another, until the light colored stripes are filled with stitching.

6. Make a ¼" tuck on both sides of each of the second color stripes (Fig. 5.9).

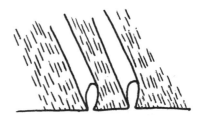

5.9 Make a ¼" tuck on both sides of each of the second color stripes.

7. Press all tucks away from embroidered stripe.

8. With the predominate Burmilana thread color, of the stripe #2 fabric, horizontally stitch two rows of 4mm long straight stitch ¼" apart, every 4", stitching the tucks down toward the unstitched stripe.

9. Halfway between the horizontal rows of stitching just stitched, stitch a single row of 4mm long straight stitch across the tucks. This time, as you stitch, open the tucks so that the folded edge of each tuck faces the embroidered stripes (Fig. 5.10). Set this fabric aside.

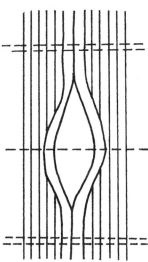

5.10 Stitch a single row of 4mm stitching across the tucks, opening the tucks as you stitch so that the folded edge of each tuck faces the embroidered stripes.

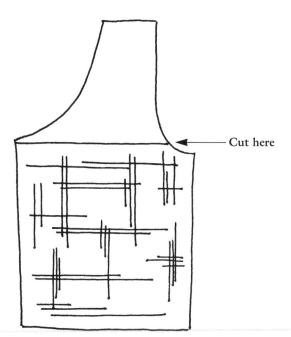

5.11 Cut the left front vest stripe across the fabric 3" above the top of the arm hole.

LOWER LEFT FRONT PANEL

1. Cut left front vest stripe #1 across the fabric 3" above top of arm hole (Fig. 5.11).

2. Cut batting to new size of lower left panel.

3. Using each of the Burmilana thread colors, sew irregular lengths of vertical and horizontal lines of straight stitching (see Fig. 5.11).

4. Cut a flower motif from the printed fabric.

5. Pin floral motif to the lower right corner of the left front of the vest, just inside the seam allowance.

6. Thread machine with Burmilana in colors that match the flower and stitch fill-in rows of forward and reverse straight stitching in the appropriate colors of the flower. Outline some portions of the flower. Leaves look great in two values of green.

7. Stitch upper left front to lower left front with right sides together, and a ½" seam allowance.

UPPER AND LOWER RIGHT FRONT PANEL OF VEST

1. With print fabric 30" long and width of top upper vest plus 1" (this is the piece of fabric described in step #12 under How To earlier in this project), make ¼" pleats in print fabric so that finished piece measures approximately 12" wide by 9" long (Fig. 5.12). Clotilde's Perfect Pleater is easy to use (see Source List). Simply tuck the fabric into every louver in the pleater, press with hot iron and allow to cool before removing fabric from pleater. Set aside with pleats in place.

5.12 Make ¼" pleats in the print fabric so that the finished piece measures approximately 12" x 9".

2. Lay right front fabric on table, right side up (stripe #1.)

3. Cut five to ten (depending on the width of the right front pattern) strips of stripes #1 and #2 the length of the vest from the 60" of stripe already pre-cut.

4. Fringe all sides of each stripe, and vary the width of the fringe from ¼" to ⅛".

5. Lay stripes vertically over right front, leaving different amounts of space between strips.

6. Weave stripe #1 and #2 horizontally, again leaving space between the strips.

7. Pin stripes in place.

8. Lay pleated flower print fabric over right front yoke. Cut away the woven stripes that are under the print fabric and discard.

9. Turn under raw edge of upper right front of pleated fabric or fringe edge and pin in place.

10. Thread sewing machine with Burmilana, matching thread to stripe color. Set straight stitch to 3.5mm long.

11. Sew vertical strips in place by stitching forward into the center of the stripe an inch or two, then push the reverse button to form the stitch pattern.

12. Repeat the stitches in step #11, only this time in the horizontal rows. Be sure to match the thread to the stripe color.

13. Use extra rows of forward and reverse stitching to blend the area where the pleated material meets the strips.

VEST BACK

1. Pin batting to wrong side of back fabric.

2. Thread machine with any color Burmilana, and set your machine to a 3.5mm long straight stitch.

3. Stitch horizontally across the fabric in forward and reverse, creating a "stippled" appearance as you sew. Repeat this process using all of the colors (Fig. 5.13).

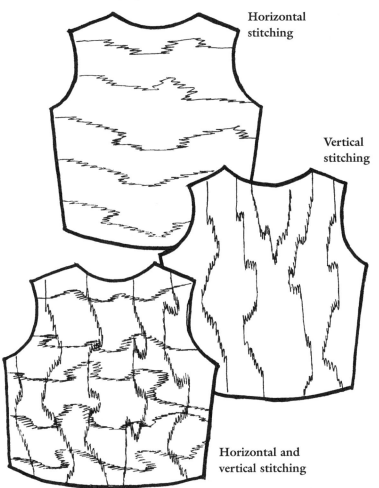

Horizontal stitching

Vertical stitching

Horizontal and vertical stitching

5.13 Using all of your thread colors, stitch horizontally and vertically across the fabric in forward and reverse to create a stippled appearance.

4. Next, using all of the Burmilana thread colors, stitch in forward and reverse across the fabric while moving the fabric vertically. Every now and then quickly change from forward to reverse. When you change from forward to reverse in a consistent rhythm, blocks of stitches will appear.

FINISHING

1. Switch to a 90/14 needle and thread bobbin and needle with construction thread.

2. Sew lining together. Lay pattern over all embroidered fabric and cut pattern to size. Sew front and back together and finish as directed by pattern.

3. Finish arm holes by using Burmilana thread (the color closest to the fabric color) to sew one row of 3.5mm long straight stitches ⅝" from edge.

FABRIC FLOWER BUTTONS

1. Using 9" x 1" of print fabric, fringe one 9" edge and pleat every ¼" on the 9" length of fabric.

2. Place the print fabric on a flat surface print side down and roll it up into a tube. This makes a flower button.

3. Straight stitch the unfringed edge of the flower with several rows of green Burmilana (Fig. 5.14).

5.14 Straight stitch the unfringed edge of the flower with several rows of green Burmilana.

4. Decide on button placement or use the buttonhole locations as marked on the pattern. Stitch to jacket at base of flowers. Use monofilament thread in needle and bobbin.

5. Repeat steps #1–#4 for the second button.

BUTTON LOOPS

1. Cut two pieces of lining fabric 7" x 1⅔". Make a ¼" fringe on each of the 1⅔" sides.

2. Fold long sides to the center, fold in half again. Press folds with fingers and pin.

3. Set the sewing machine for a 2.5mm straight stitch and stitch both long edges ⅛" from edge. Use a 90/14 needle and balanced tensions in the needle and bobbin.

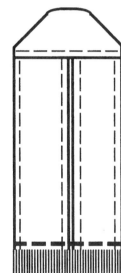

4. Fold in half so that the fringed edges lay parallel to each other (Fig. 5.15).

5. Fold the folded end to form a point and straight stitch through the base.

6. Decide on placement of buttonholes. Measure 1¼" from edge of vest front, pin the fringed end of the buttonhole here with the point off the fabric.

5.15 Fold the button loop fabric in half so that the fringed edges lay parallel to each other.

7. Stitch in place just inside both fringed edges and on outer edge of the loop that is pinned to the vest.

Straight stitch in embroidery is a creative tool. As you move along to Chapter Six: Embellishing with the Zigzag Stitch, you will combine zigzag with straight stitch to multiply your machine embroidery possibilities.

6 Chapter Six

Embellishing with the Zigzag Stitch

Exciting Ideas to Turn Simple Zigzags into Creative Designs

Do not let what you cannot do interfere with what you can do.

—John Wooden,
college basketball coach

While the zigzag, or swing needle, sewing machine was invented in the late 1800s, the homemaker had to wait more than fifty years to have a zigzag sewing machine. In the 1940s the first zigzags were purchased by our mothers and grandmothers. A great many people thought that a serge of creativeness would ensue, but instead, the ordinary homemaker viewed the zigzag as a utility stitch and engaged in little creative embellishment.

Today, embellishment with the sewing machine has gathered great interest and because of the zigzag needle the range of embellishment is enormous. In this chapter we will explore some ordinary and some extraordinary uses for this very versatile stitch.

ZIGZAG WITH THE PRESSER FOOT

Embellishment is easy to do with nothing more than a zigzag stitch and a presser foot. The following project is a snap. Go ahead, give it a try.

Four Way Zigzag Make-up Bag

(see color section)

Zigzag stitch can turn into a plaid or a tweed when stitched in four directions. Either choose multi-color or four different colors of rayon

6.1 It's easy to create plaids and tweeds by machine embroidering on the horizontal, the vertical, and the diagonal.

thread and sew in four directions—vertical, horizontal, right to left, and left to right. You will be pleasantly surprised by the texture and pattern produced (Fig. 6.1).

Supplies

- One spool of multi-color 40 wt rayon or four different colors of 40 wt rayon plus an additional spool of bright, high contrast 40 wt rayon

- One spool of bobbin thread for machine embroidery

- 10" x 12" medium to heavy weight fabric

- 10" x 12" stabilizer

- 100/16 needle

- 70/10 or 60/8 sewing machine needles for attaching beads

- Embroidery presser foot

- Zipper presser foot

- 7" zipper

- A few seed beads to complement thread

- Monofilament thread

HOW TO

1. Prepare machine thread and 100/16 needle and bobbin.

2. Decrease needle tension by one number.

3. Activate the needle down feature if possible.

4. Place stabilizer under fabric and position both under the needle.

5. Set zigzag to 4mm wide and 1mm long.

6. Cover the fabric with abutting vertical rows of zigzag. If you are using the needle down feature, the needle will be down in the fabric at the

end of each row. If you do not have the needle down feature, use the hand wheel to place the needle in the down position, then simply turn the fabric 180 degrees to stitch the next row.

7. If you have chosen four different rayon colors, change thread color in the needle after finishing all of the vertical rows and after finishing stitching in each direction, horizontal and diagonal. If you are using the multi-color thread, continue using it for the entire project. The sample uses four colors of rayon instead of multi-colored thread with a fifth color for a final accent.

8. Next cover the fabric horizontally with zigzag.

9. Then finish by stitching in two more directions: First, diagonally right to left. Second, diagonally left to right. This sequence of direction gives a plaidlike pattern with multi-color thread.

Hint

If you do the diagonal stitching first, followed by vertical and horizontal rows, the result will be a more on-grain, mottled effect when using the multi-color thread.

10. If you have chosen to embroider with four different colors of rayon, now finish the embroidery by sewing seven rows of abutting zigzag diagonally from upper right corner to lower left corner. You may want to use a contrasting color.

11. Prepare to attach the beads by choosing a needle with a shaft small enough to fit in the bead hole (70/10 or 60/8). Thread your needle and bobbin with monofilament thread, which will not be visible once the bead is attached. If your bobbin is plastic, remember to fill it only halfway to prevent bobbin breakage. If you prefer, you may use the rayon embroidery thread in the bobbin instead.

12. Set machine to straight stitch with a balanced tension.

13. Remove the presser foot and lower the feed dogs.

14. Fold fabric side seams together to determine bead placement (sometimes it is easiest to mark their placement using a water-soluble pen). Lay area to be beaded flat on bed of sewing machine under needle.

15. Lower the presser bar and take one stitch. Bring the bobbin thread to the surface.

16. Take several straight stitches in place.

17. Center machine needle over spot where a bead is to be. Thread a single bead onto the shaft of the needle. Take a stitch. The bead is now stitched securely in place (Fig. 6.2).

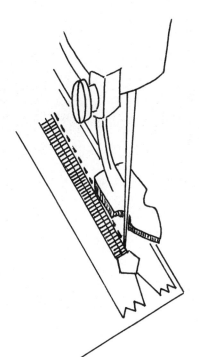

6.3 Lay zipper face down on the right side of the fabric, keeping the edge even with the fabric. Stitch in place.

6.2 To attach a bead, position the sewing machine needle over the fabric, thread a single bead onto the needle shaft, and take a stitch.

18. Using free motion straight stitches, move the fabric so the needle is over the next spot where a bead is needed and repeat.

19. Raise the feed dogs to finish the bag.

FINISHING

1. To insert the zipper, install zipper presser foot.

2. Lay zipper face down on right side of fabric, edge even with fabric. Stitch in place (Fig. 6.3).

3. Fold zipper to wrong side of fabric. Edge stitch fabric close to zipper (Fig. 6.4).

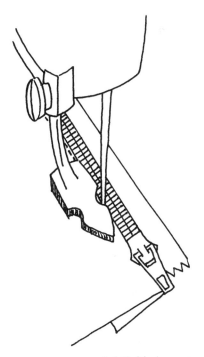

6.4 Fold zipper to wrong side of fabric and edge stitch fabric close to the zipper.

4. Repeat steps #2 and #3 with the other side of the zipper and the fabric.

5. Unzip zipper and turn bag inside out.

6. Sew side seams with ½" seam allowance and cut off excess zipper.

7. Turn bag right side out.

ZIGZAG AS COUCHING

Couching is a decorative method whereby a thread is arranged attractively on a fabric and attached by means of another thread. This second thread can be identical to the couched thread or provide constrast. The attaching stitches cross over the top of the couched thread at even intervals. Couching, long used in hand embroidery, is a natural use of the zigzag stitch.

Patchwork Pin Cushion

(see color section)

 MACHINE PATCHWORK A SMALL SQUARE OF FABRIC OR PURCHASE PREPRINTED PATCHWORK MATERIAL. THIS CHARMING PIN CUSHION USES THE TECHNIQUE OF COUCHING.

Supplies

- Patchwork or patchwork-like fabric and fabric for back of pin cushion, each approximately 8" x 8"
- Batting 8" x 8"
- Three yards of 4mm wide metallic braid
- Four handfuls of polyester stuffing to fill the pin cushion
- 90/14 needle
- One spool of Monofil
- Construction thread to sew pin cushion together

HOW TO

1. Layer patchwork fabric over batting.

2. Thread a 90/14 needle and bobbin with Monofil.

3. Set sewing machine to 4mm wide zigzag with balanced tensions.

4. Lay 4mm wide metallic braid over real or printed seam of patchwork, beginning at an outside edge. Couch the metallic braid in place with the zigzag stitch. At the end of a seam bend the braid and follow another seam line until all are covered. Bending the braid at each intersection helps eliminate fraying and waste. The dark line in Figure 6.5 shows a possible path for the metallic braid. End the braid on an outside edge of the design. The needle down position is helpful when turning corners.

5. Remove the fabric from the machine and place it right side up. Place the fabric for the back of the pin cushion right side down over the embellished fabric. Pin in place at the edge

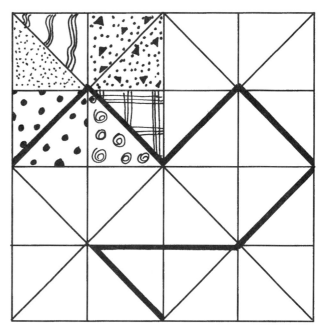

6.5 Couch the metallic braid with the zigzag stitch, making sure to follow the patchwork "seams" as you go. End the braid on an outside edge of the design.

of the design leaving a 2"–3" opening on one side. Sew together with construction thread, making sure the ends of the braid are hidden from sight by the seam attaching the front and back fabrics together.

6. Turn right side out, stuff, and slip stitch opening closed with construction thread.

This couching technique can be used with a larger quilted block for a pillow or with several quilted squares to make a garment or wall hanging.

Sequin Waste Christmas Cards

FOR THOSE OF YOU WHO HAVE NEVER HEARD OF IT, SEQUIN WASTE IS THE SHEET OF METALLIC LOOKING, PLASTIC-LIKE MATERIAL LEFT OVER AFTER SEQUINS HAVE BEEN MACHINE PRESSED AND CUT OUT OF IT. Look for rolls of this shiny, holey material in craft stores. Christmas wreath bows look terrific when made out of sequin waste as do Christmas cards decorated with sequin waste cut in the shape of ornaments and attached with a zigzag stitch (Figs. 6.6 and 6.7).

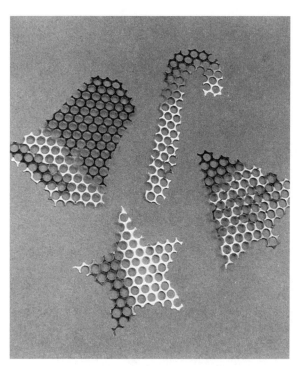

6.7 Sequin waste can be cut into a variety of shapes to suit every holiday and special occasion.

6.6 Sequin waste Christmas Tree Card.

Supplies

- Blank cards with matching envelopes

- Sequin waste

- Tear away stabilizer the size of the front panel of the card

- 40 wt metallic thread

- 100/16 needle

- Tape that can be removed easily without tearing the paper

- Darning foot

HOW TO

1. Enlarge pattern as necessary to fit the card (see the patterns at the end of this chapter and refer to "Enlarging and Reducing Designs" in Chapter Four).

2. Cut Christmas pattern from sequin waste. Lay stabilizer under front panel of card and center sequin waste shape on front of card. Tape in place.

3. Thread a 100/16 needle and bobbin with metallic thread. The needle and bobbin tensions should be balanced.

4. Set sewing machine for widest zigzag, at least 6mm wide.

5. Activate the needle down position if you have it. If not, be sure to end each set of four zigzag stitches by using the hand wheel to move the needle to its lowest position.

6. Attach the darning foot. Lower or cover the feed dogs.

7. Lay card on bed of the sewing machine and use the hand wheel to bring the needle down through the center of one of the holes of the sequin waste. Bring the bobbin thread to the surface. Take four zigzag stitches in the same place, and be sure to center the zags in the adjacent hole. Repeat this until all holes of the sequin waste are covered.

8. Trim threads and stabilizer around edge of stitching and mail to someone you love.

CORDS, CORDS, AND MORE CORDS

Making cords with the sewing machine is an adventure you won't want to miss. All sizes are possible. Some cords are made of a base of thread, others have upholstery cord as their base,

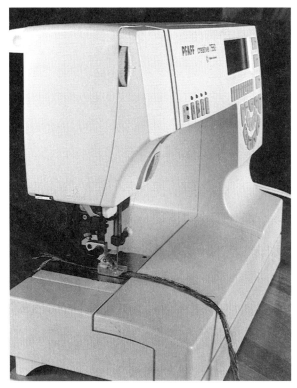

6.8 Making cords on the sewing machine is easy and fun.

and still others have string or yarn. It is easiest to use a presser foot with a large concave cutout on the underside of the foot (Fig. 6.9). Check your sewing machine manual to see if a grooved foot is available. If not see step #3 below.

6.9 Use a presser foot with a large concave cutout on the bottom when making cords.

After the cords are made there is no end to their uses. In this section we will be using cords to make jewelry and a belt. Other ideas include couching the cords on clothing and using them as texture in an embroidery.

Here are some general directions for making cording.

1. Set the sewing machine to the widest zigzag stitch with a satin stitch length of .35mm. Needle and bobbin tensions should be balanced.

2. Lay the base cord under the concave presser

foot and stitch with a moderate speed. Often it is necessary to make a second row of stitching over the first to obtain complete coverage.

3. If there is no concave presser foot you can be successful making cording in the free motion embroidery mode. Remove the presser foot and lower the feed dogs. Use a large needle, size 100/16. Put the base for the cord under the needle, lower the presser bar, and take six to eight straight stitches into the base cord to anchor the sewing thread. Reset the sewing machine for the widest zigzag stitch and the stitch length at zero. Then proceed as in step #2. Remember that in the free motion mode you must move the thread base under the needle away from you as the stitches are formed. End by returning the stitch width to zero and taking six to eight straight stitches.

Hints

- In the free motion mode it is mandatory that the cord base thread lay flat on the bed of the sewing machine. If the base thread is lifted above the bed it will cause the needle thread to rub on the base and break.

- When making cording in the free motion mode it is easy to move the base cord toward you and restitch an area that is not completely covered with stitching. When the area is covered, reverse direction and again move the base cord away from you to continue stitching a new area.

Necklace Cords
(see color section)

 AFTER MAKING THIS SIMPLE NECK-LACE YOU MAY WANT TO EMBROI-DER SEVERAL CORDS AND COMBINE THEM BY WEAVING OR BRAIDING.

HOW TO

1. Thread 100/16 needle with metallic thread. Use 40 wt rayon in the bobbin to create a candy stripe effect or use the same thread in both the needle and the bobbin for a solid color necklace.

2. Decide whether to use a concave presser foot or the free motion embroidery mode and set the stitch width and length accordingly.

3 Make sure that both needle and bobbin tensions are balanced.

4. Gather the seven to ten strands of cotton embroidery floss and lay them under the needle. Begin stitching with a straight stitch 5" from the end to anchor the sewing thread. Change to the widest zigzag, and as stitching begins be sure all

strands of embroidery floss are included in each swing of the needle. Embroider the floss, covering it completely except for the last 5".

5. Thread beads by hand onto the ends of the floss, tying knots between each bead and after the last bead.

6. Tie both ends together with an overhand knot starting 2" from the end of the embroidery.

Supplies

- Seven to ten strands of cotton embroidery floss 42" long

- Metallic and rayon 40 wt machine embroidery thread

- 100/16 needle

- Concave presser foot or none (see free motion cord making #3 above)

- An assortment of various size beads to complement the floss and thread

The Bundle Belt
(see color section)

 IN THIS PROJECT THE CORDS ARE EMBROIDERED AND THEN BRAIDED IN GROUPS OF THREE. Choose at least one metallic, a bright rayon, and a subdued rayon. The sample uses two rayons and two metallics.

Supplies

- 40 wt machine embroidery thread in four colors (at least one should be metallic)

- Upholstery cording the length of your waist plus 6", multiplied by nine and then increased by 20" (for example, a 30" waist would require 344" (28⅔ ft) of cording)

- 8" x 8¼" fabric to match one of the colors of thread or the garment the belt is to go with

- Garment construction thread the color of the fabric

- One large button

- Concave presser foot or none and an embroidery presser foot

- 100/16 needle

HOW TO

1. Measure 20" of upholstery cording and mark that point. Now divide the remainder of the cord into nine equal pieces. Cut the cord so that there are nine pieces, with one piece 20" longer than the others.

2. Embroider the cords by following the general cording directions and the directions for the corded necklace. Begin at one end of the upholstery cord and embroider the entire cord.

3. Using the most important color thread, embroider three cords; include among these three cords the one cord that is 20" longer than the others.

4. Embroider two cords of each of the other three colors of thread (six cords).

FINISHING

1. Gather cord in groups of three. The cord that is 20" longer than the rest needs to be centered in one group of three so that 10" hang on each end and are not part of the braid (Fig. 6.10). Braid the three groups of cord beginning 5" from the end. End the braid 5" from other end.

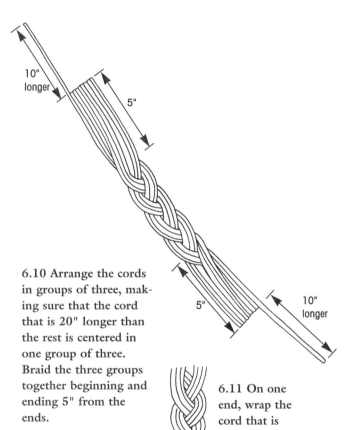

6.10 Arrange the cords in groups of three, making sure that the cord that is 20" longer than the rest is centered in one group of three. Braid the three groups together beginning and ending 5" from the ends.

6.11 On one end, wrap the cord that is longer than the rest around the remaining cords and knot it.

2. Wrap the 10" long cord around the other cords starting at the end of the braided cords (Fig. 6.11). To secure the cord bring the end over and under the

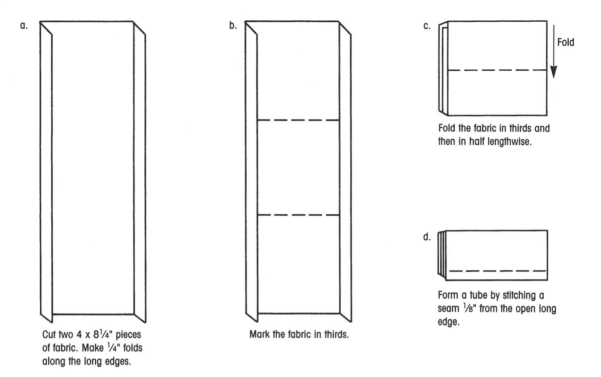

a. Cut two 4 x 8¼" pieces of fabric. Make ¼" folds along the long edges.

b. Mark the fabric in thirds.

c. Fold the fabric in thirds and then in half lengthwise.

d. Form a tube by stitching a seam ⅛" from the open long edge.

6.12 Making the fabric covering for the closure.

last wrap. Pull the knot tight and toward remaining ends.

3. Leaving one cord long to form the loop for the button, cut the rest to measure 3" from the last wrap at the base of the knot. If none of the remaining cords are long enough to form a loop, embroider a short piece of upholstery cord in any color, making it long enough to make a loop for the button. Repeat wrap and knot on other end.

4. To create the cover for the closure, cut fabric in half so that each piece is 4" x 8¼". Make a ¼" fold on the long edges, wrong sides together (Fig. 6.12a). Fold fabric in thirds (Fig. 6.12b). Fold in half lengthwise, right sides together (Fig 6.12c). Stitch a seam with garment construction thread and an embroidery presser foot, ⅛" from the open long edge, forming a tube (Fig. 6.12d). Turn right side out.

5. Pull fabric tube over cord ends. Seam should be at center and the back of the belt.

6. Spread the cords so they lay flat next to each other. Adjust fabric tube so that it begins 1" from knotted wrap. Stitch fabric in place by stitching through cords and fabric ⅛" from the end of the fabric nearest the wrapped cords.

7. Form a loop large enough for the button with covered cord. Stitch centered loop in place through fabric and cord ¹⁄₁₆" from end of fabric (Fig. 6.13).

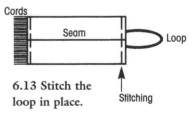

Cords   Seam   Loop

Stitching

6.13 Stitch the loop in place.

8. Finish other end the same except do not form the loop. Cut all cords 3" long.

9. Attach button to non-looped end.

ZIGZAG WITH TAILOR TACKING FOOT

The fringe or tailor tacking foot makes an intriguing embroidery tool with many quick and creative uses. Although designed to be used as a pattern marking tool, it may be used as a presser foot to develop texture in any design, whether in a confined area or a large open space.

Hints

To successfully use the tailor tacking foot, keep the following points in mind.

• You must always use a zigzag stitch when using the tailor tacking foot because of the bar in the center of the foot.

• Set the sewing machine to zigzag before you attach the foot.

• Never try to use the hand wheel while the presser foot is in the up position because the needle cannot clear the bar of the foot. If you need to use the hand wheel while using this foot, always lower the presser bar. Wait until the machine stops and the needle is in the up position before raising the presser foot.

• Stop the machine and push the fabric away from you when a corner needs to be navigated. This removes the threads on the bar of the foot. After removing the threads on the bar, turn the fabric and begin stitching in the new direction where the stitches ended.

• The fringe/tailor tacking foot creates fragile stitches that easily pull out of the fabric if they are not stabilized by fabric glue and another piece of fabric on the back of the embroidery. Be careful when using iron on interfacing because the ironing will change the texture of the embroidery and interfere with its design.

• Do not try to stitch in reverse!

Hearts to Give

HERE ROWS OF TAILOR TACKING STITCH FORM A SOLID DESIGN OF TEXTURED THREAD.

6.14 Hearts to Give.

Supplies

• Rayon and metallic 40 wt machine embroidery thread

• White or black machine embroidery bobbin thread depending on the color of the card

• 90/14 needle

• 8" x 8" piece of heavy weight fabric such as denim, or medium weight fabric and two layers of medium weight stabilizer

• Pattern (see heart pattern at the end of the chapter or use one of your own)

• Greeting card with matlike opening; use either a heart shaped or a rectangular opening

• Clear tape

• Water-soluble pen to transfer design

• Fringe/tailor tacking presser foot

HOW TO

1. Thread needle with both the rayon and the metallic threads. Use machine embroidery bobbin thread in the bobbin.

Hint

On most machines two threads are threaded as though they were a single thread except at the tension disks, where the two threads go on either side of the tension disk. The two threads may be separated a second time just above the needle: use both thread guides if they are available. Consult your sewing machine manual for exact directions.

---

2. Use a balanced tension in the bobbin and decrease the needle tension by two numbers or until no bobbin thread comes to the surface.

3. Engage the needle down position if available. If not, at a corner or angle in the embroidery, use the hand wheel to lower the needle into the fabric.

4. Insert new 90/14 needle, set the machine to 3.5mm wide zigzag, and the satin stitch length (.40mm). Consult your sewing machine manual for tension requirements.

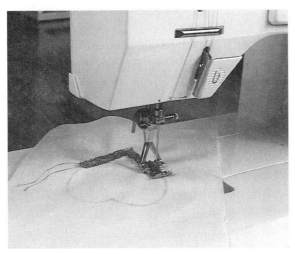

6.15 Using a 3.5mm wide zigzag, stitch the outline of the heart design.

5. Enlarge pattern if necessary to fit card (see "Enlarging and Reducing Designs" in Chapter Four). Trace pattern in the center of the fabric. Other shape outlines can easily be used: candy canes, bells, animals, pumpkins, shamrocks, and flowers.

6. Attach fringe/tailor tacking foot.

7. Stitch the outline of the heart design. Begin on either straight side of the heart near the base of the heart (Fig. 6.15). When you reach the angle in the heart, leave the needle in the fabric, raise the presser foot, remove the threads from the bar of the foot and change direction. Lower the presser foot and begin stitching in the new direction, following the pattern until the first row is covered with stitches.

8. For the second row only, remove the rayon thread from the sewing machine and change the stitch length to .35mm. Sew the second row abutting the first row. This will add a solid row of metallic thread in the design, thereby adding visual interest.

9. Change the length back to .40mm and rethread the machine with both the rayon and the metallic. Complete all the remaining rows until the entire area is filled.

FINISHING

1. Clip long threads at the beginning and end.

2. Cut fabric ½" smaller than the outer edge of the card and tape in place. If the card does not come in three sections, cut a piece of paper the color of, or contrasting with, the embroidery and tape it in place, covering the entire back of the embroidery. The tape will hold the embroidery in place on the card and at the same time secure the stitches. After the fringe stitches are secured in place with tape or glue, it is possible to create a tufted look by clipping some or all of the loops.

Thread Flocked Table Trees for the Holidays

 THREE FREE-STANDING TEXTURED TREES ADORNED WITH RED BEADS COMPLETE THE FESTIVE LOOK CREATED WITH THE "FESTIVE TABLE FROCK" IN CHAPTER SEVEN. This project also uses the tailor tacking presser foot to create texture (Fig. 6.16).

6.16 Thread Flocked Table Tree.

HOW TO

1. Reproduce on white paper each of the three tree patterns at the back of this chapter, making sure to double their size. Then transfer four tree patterns of each size to green fabric. Use any of the enlarging and transferring techniques in Chapter Four.

2. Thread sewing machine needle with both the green rayon and the gold metallic. (See the hint in "Hearts to Give" for threading two threads in one needle.)

3. Thread bobbin with machine embroidery bobbin thread.

4. Use a balanced tension in the bobbin and decrease the needle tension by two numbers or until no bobbin thread comes to the surface. Set machine at 3.5mm wide zigzag and satin stitch length .40mm. Bring the bobbin thread up to the bed of the sewing machine. Attach the fringe/tailor tacking foot.

5. Pin two layers of stabilizer to the underside of the green fabric. Begin stitching on the traced line at the bottom of the large tree. When you reach the first branch stop the machine and raise

Supplies

- Cardboard 22" x 17"

- ½ yard of 45" wide, medium weight green fabric (same color as green thread)

- One yard of medium weight tear away stabilizer

- 1000 meter spools of 40 wt tree green rayon and gold metallic

- Fringe/tailor tacking foot

- Glue gun and fifteen glue sticks

- 1000 meter spool of white machine embroidery bobbin thread

- 100/16 needle

- Approximately 150 3mm red beads plus three large, red, ornate beads for tree tops

- One small gold bead and two medium size gold beads for tree tops

- Fifteen yards of gold craft thread, either smooth (Glamour color #2425) or whiskered (Frizz color #15)

- Hand needle that accommodates both the beads and the gold craft thread the presser foot, remove the threads from the bar of the foot, turn the fabric in the new direction up the tree, lower the presser foot and begin stitching again. Stitch the entire outline of the tree.

6. Abut the second and all other rows to the previous row of stitching. Push the previous row of fringe to the right as you stitch each row. Fill the entire area of the tree with fringe stitch.

7. Stitch four trees of each size as described in steps #5 and #6

FINISHING

1. From the cardboard, cut out two tree shapes of each size tree. Be sure to include the center

dot on each cardboard shape.

2. On one tree of each size of the cardboard trees cut an ⅛" slot through the cardboard from the center dot to the point of the tree. On the other tree of the same size cut an ⅛" slot from the center dot down to the base of the tree.

3. Put the tree with the center cut from the dot down over the tree cut from the dot up. Center the tree tops. The cardboard tree is now free standing (Fig. 6.17).

4. Cut the fabric around each of the embroidered trees as close as possible without cutting into the embroidery.

5. Spread hot glue into one center angle of the

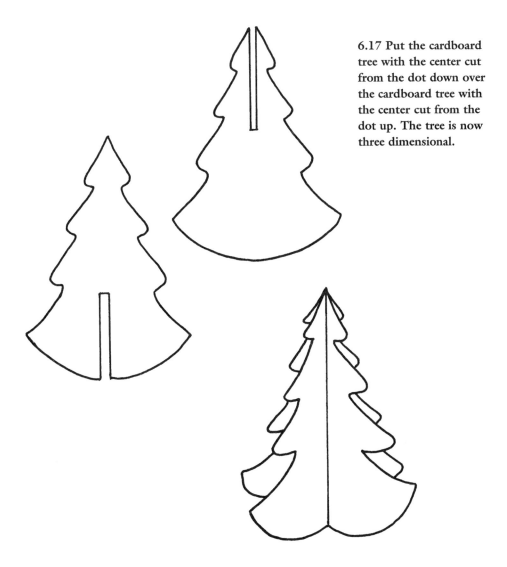

6.17 Put the cardboard tree with the center cut from the dot down over the cardboard tree with the center cut from the dot up. The tree is now three dimensional.

6.18 Spread hot glue into one center angle of the cardboard tree (a). Center and press the embroidered tree into the glued angle (b).

6.19 Use a hand needle to attach gold craft thread and red beads to the branches of the tree.

cardboard tree (Fig. 6.18a). Center and press the embroidered tree into the glued angle (Fig. 6.18b). Repeat by gluing a second embroidered tree into an adjoining angle.

6. Start at the top of the tree and apply a small amount of hot glue to the top branch edges of the cardboard that adjoin both embroidered trees. Press the embroidery from both sides of the cardboard into the glue so that a nice finished edge is obtained.

7. Repeat the gluing of the center of the tree and edges until all the branches are attached.

8 Thread gold craft thread (45" for large tree, 36" for medium tree and 28" for small tree) in hand needle. Knot end and sew to attach the thread on the tree top. With the thread still through the needle, thread three red beads for the large tree. (For the medium tree thread two red beads and for the small tree thread one red bead.) Then lay the thread over a top branch and take one stitch into the point. Add another bead

or beads and stitch through the next point down (Fig. 6.19). Repeat through the bottom point. When you reach the bottom, bring the gold craft thread under the tree along the edge and across to the opposite bottom branch. Take a stitch into the point, add bead(s) as before, and continue up the tree. Take several sewing stitches at the top of the tree and then clip thread.

9. With a second thread embellish the remaining two edges.

10 At tree centers string beads randomly using two strands in the small tree and three strands in the medium and large trees. Attach strings of beads to tree top.

11. Sew random beads on top of tree dripping over the edge.

12. Hand sew red ornate bead to top of tree, add gold bead, and bring the needle down through the center of the large bead. Take several tacking stitches by hand and clip thread.

13. Add some hot glue under the large red bead for stability.

14. Finish the two remaining trees in same manner. Three trees grouped together complete the elegant "Festive Table Frock" in Chapter Seven.

USING ZIGZAG STITCH TO COVER CANVAS

Canvas embroidery, commonly stitched by hand, can be transferred to machine embroidery easily by using the zigzag stitch. The word canvas refers to the ground fabric to which the threads are applied. It may actually be canvas or another type of fabric altogether, but regardless of the type of ground used, it must be even in weave and easily counted. Usually the canvas weave has a hole between each thread. The basic process involved in this type of embroidery is that the needle enters (zigs) a given hole, skips over the prescribed number of holes, and (zags) into the next prescribed hole. This step is repeated three to four times in the same pair of holes as directed, then the canvas is moved and the zigzag is repeated in the next set of holes.

Zig and Zag Bargello Coin Purse
(see color section)

ANYONE WHO DOES HAND WORKED BARGELLO, A TYPE OF CANVAS WORK IN WHICH A WAVE PATTERN IS CREATED (FIG. 6.20), WILL BE HARD PRESSED TO NOTICE THAT YOUR LITTLE PURSE HAS BEEN EMBROIDERED BY MACHINE IN ONE QUARTER THE TIME.

A simple arch pattern has been chosen for this coin purse, but you will find many, many patterns for Bargello in needlepoint books available at your local library, bookstore, or needlework library. You will be charmed by the number of projects possible with this technique.

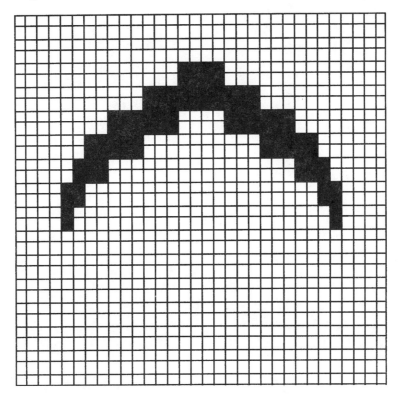

6.20 The pattern for the Zig and Zag Bargello Coin Purse creates a wavelike design.

Supplies

- 9½" x 5" #18 mono canvas (see Source List)

- Four spools of Burmilana thread #12 in four colors

- One spool of machine embroidery bobbin thread

- One spool of monofilament

- Darning presser foot and regular presser foot

- 110/18 needle

- Light to medium weight lining material 9½" x 5"

- One button ½"–¾" in diameter

- 6" of thread covered elastic for loop closure

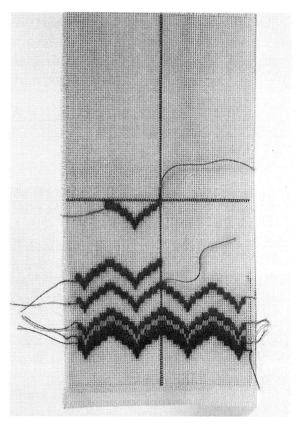

6.21 Begin stitching on the center line of the canvas.

HOW TO

1. Insert 100/18 needle, and thread needle and bobbin with garment construction thread. Set machine at 4mm wide, 1mm long zigzag and stitch around the entire edge of the canvas. This will prevent the canvas from unraveling.

2. Attach darning foot and lower feed dogs. Decrease needle tension by two numbers. Fill bobbin with machine embroidery bobbin thread.

3. Set machine on straight stitch.

4. Arrange Burmilana thread colors in the order they will be used. Thread machine needle with first color of Burmilana.

5. Find the center of the canvas both lengthwise and widthwise by folding the canvas lightly. Mark the center lines with a permanent marker.

6. Place needle several holes above center line and take several straight stitches to secure the thread (Fig. 6.21). Cut needle thread end close to canvas.

7. Reset sewing machine to either a 4mm or a 4.5mm wide zigzag, whichever width zags into the fourth hole. Begin stitching on the center line of the canvas, holding the canvas horizontally under the needle so that the first stitch of the pattern enters the hole on the center line. Zig into the first hole as indicated (see Fig. 6.21). Then zag into the fourth hole down. Stitch three complete zigzags in each hole.

8. Move the canvas towards you one hole, and repeat. Now you have two complete stitches side by side.

9. Move the canvas towards you one hole and **down** two holes.

10. Make three complete sets of zigzag stitches (zag into the fourth hole down).

11. Move the canvas towards you one hole and down two holes.

12. Following the pattern, make three complete sets of stitches. A single complete pattern is three zigzag stitches in one pair of holes. Move the canvas towards you one hole and down two holes. Make two complete stitches. Again, move the canvas towards you one hole and down two holes. Make one complete stitch. Move the canvas towards you one hole and down two holes. Make one more complete stitch. You have now completed one half of a pattern.

13. Continue stitching by moving over one hole and **up** two holes, repeating the graph pattern as seen in Fig. 6.21. By moving the canvas up the formation of the arch is begun.

14. Complete the pattern and repeat it until only three to four holes remain before the edge of the canvas is reached. Switch the machine to straight stitch and stitch through the last three to four holes to the very edge.

15. Move the canvas back to the center and complete the pattern from the center of the canvas to the other edge. Leave three to four holes empty on this side of the canvas as well. Switch the machine to straight stitch and stitch through the last three to four holes to the very edge.

Hint

Stitching the first row is the most difficult. All following rows follow the pattern of this first row.

16. Change thread color and begin the second row at the edge of the canvas furthest from you. As you begin stitching the second row, stitch into the fourth hole of the previous row of stitches and then zag three holes away (four counting the hole the needle is in) into previously unstitched canvas. Complete the row across the canvas following the arch made by the first row.

17. Change thread color and do the third and fourth rows, changing to a new color thread after each row.

18. Repeat pattern and color change until the canvas is covered.

19. Fill in partial rows created by the arch design at the top and bottom of the canvas.

20. Press on wrong side with a steam iron.

FINISHING

1. Thread machine needle and bobbin with monofilament thread. Make sure the needle and bobbin thread tensions are balanced. Attach regular presser foot and raise feed dogs.

2. Lay lining fabric right side down on the right side of the embroidery. Set sewing machine to 2.5mm long straight stitch. Stitch both long sides of the embroidery and lining together with a ¼" seam allowance (Fig. 6.22).

6.22 Using the regular presser foot, stitch both long sides of the embroidery and lining together with a ¼" seam allowance.

3. Turn right side out and press.

4. Turn both unsewn ends in ½" and press.

5. Decide which end will be the front. Make a button loop of the elastic and pin it in place, making sure that it is centered and between the lining and the embroidered canvas.

6.23 Stitch both ends closed as close to the edge as possible.

6. Stitch both ends closed as close to the edge as possible (Fig. 6.23).

7. Fold the canvas in thirds in the shape of a purse. Place the button in the center of the end that does not have the button loop. Stitch the button in place by hand.

8. Stitch side of purse together with ¼" seam allowance with 2.5mm long straight stitch and monofilament thread in the needle and the bobbin (Fig. 6.24).

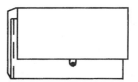

6.24 Use a 2.5mm long straight stitch to stitch side of purse together with a ¼" seam allowance.

USING ZIGZAG STITCH IN FREE MOTION EMBROIDERY

Remember when you used free motion embroidery with the straight stitch and found new freedom because you were able to stitch in any direction instead of just forward and reverse?

Using zigzag stitch in the free motion mode also allows you to stitch in any direction but with a big difference. When stitching free motion zigzag in forward and reverse (away from you and toward you) the stitches will resemble a normal looking zigzag or satin stitch. But if you move the fabric to the right or left as you zigzag, the stitches will form a straight line. Likewise, if you move the fabric at an angle, a partial zigzag stitch will form. For example, a free motion zigzag stitch at 30° looks like a full straight stitch while a zigzag stitch at a 45° angle is a straight line (Fig. 6.25). Practice on a scrap of fabric using a machine embroidery hoop and stabilizer. You may want to return to the exercise for free motion embroidery in Chapter Five and complete it in zigzag stitch.

The dimensions of designs change dramatically when using zigzag in the free motion embroidery mode. Because there is more variety in the width of the stitch, curved lines can be pencil thin, narrow, or as wide as the sewing machine can make them. Design possibilities continue to multiply when you consider stitch density, which allows for variation from a very open stitch to a stitch where the stitches abut.

6.25 Zigzag stitches sewn at various angles.

Long and Short Stitch

 LONG AND SHORT STITCH IS THE BLENDING STITCH DONE IN CREWEL EMBROIDERY TO ALLOW FOR GRADUAL CHANGE OF COLOR. It is especially useful when embroidering flowers and petals. The outside edge of a petal is started by stitching a long stitch, followed by a short stitch varied in length one half to one quarter the length of the long stitch. This is repeated on the entire outside edge of the petal. Now that you understand the process try a petal or two.

6.26 Long and Short Stitch Sampler.

HOW TO

1. Hoop a scrap of medium weight fabric in a solid color. Transfer to the fabric the leaf and petal designs at the end of the chapter (refer back to Chapter Four for directions for transferring fabric). Place two layers of medium weight stabilizer under the fabric. Put all layers in a machine embroidery hoop.

2. Thread a 110/18 universal needle with Burmilana in a floral shade, either the lightest or the darkest value of all of the blues or pinks or purples or reds that you have. Thread the bobbin with white machine embroidery bobbin thread.

3. Set sewing machine on straight stitch. Engage the needle down feature. If you do not have a needle down feature simply rotate the hand wheel, moving the needle into the fabric when needed.

4. Decrease the needle tension by two numbers.

5. Use the darning foot and lower the feed dogs.

6. Position the petal on its side with the base to the right and tip to the left. Lower the presser bar. Take a single stitch at the base of the petal and pull on the needle thread to bring the bobbin thread to the surface. Take four to five more straight stitches to secure the thread and then cut the needle and bobbin threads ends away.

7. Set the machine to 4mm zigzag, zero length.

Supplies

- 6" machine embroidery hoop
- 8" x 8" solid color, medium weight fabric
- Water-soluble pen
- 16" x 16" medium weight stabilizer
- One spool each of three flower colors and three leaf colors
- Darning presser foot
- 110/18 needle
- One spool white machine embroidery bobbin thread
- Leaf and petal pattern (see pattern at end of chapter)

Beginning at the base of the petal, run the machine at a moderate speed and stitch irregularly across the base edge. Use the zigzag stitch as a pencil line stitching horizontally from the base of the petal in the direction of the tip. Return to the beginning and stitch a second row of 4mm wide zigzag satin stitch across the base of the petal on the outside edge to give a smooth edge.

8. Change to the next value of color (the shade nearest the first one used). With this color zig into the tips of the previous row and zag out into the open space. Vary the lengths of the zigs and zags to emulate the color change of a real flower petal. Be especially aware of the contour of the petal. When stitching an entire flower change colors to reflect value (light or dark) change as its petals abut or partially cover other petals. Continue changing color, getting either progressively darker or lighter. Three to five color changes in each petal are realistic. When embroidering an entire flower complete all of the outside edges of all of the petals before changing to the next color value.

9. Smooth the tip edge of the petal by stitching a row of 4mm wide zigzag.

10. Next try a leaf by free motion zigzagging at the tip and following the outside edge with a random, jagged stitch. The stitch needs to aim toward the center vein. When you reach the base of the stem leave the needle down in the fabric and turn the hoop so that the hoop is in position to zig into the outside edge and zag downward toward the center vein and base of the leaf.

11. With the machine in the straight stitch mode fill in the stem.

Now that you have practiced a leaf and a petal try the following design.

Machine Crewelled Mums

MANY OF MY FRIENDS WHO DO HAND EMBROIDERY HAVE BEEN FOOLED BY THIS MACHINE EMBROIDERED PIECE. They do not believe that I did it on my sewing machine in one quarter of the time it would have taken me to embroider it by hand. The use of Burmilana, a wool/acrylic thread, in the needle and a regular machine embroidery thread in the bobbin creates the crewel look. A little practice will allow you to perfect the shading techniques.

Authentic crewel embroidery is most often done on tightly woven, 100% linen fabric. A neutral color will be the easiest to work with as it will make color choices less difficult. You may wish to review the information on hooping fabric in Chapter Four. Tightly hooped fabric is especially important when using the heavy wool/acrylic thread in the needle along with the zigzag stitch since both tend to pull the fabric in the direction of the dense stitches. The fabric will be sure to pucker if it hasn't been pulled tight in the hoop.

6.27 Machine Crewelled Mums.

Supplies

- Medium to heavy weight 10" x 12" linen fabric

- Two 10" x 12" pieces of medium weight stabilizer

- White machine embroidery bobbin thread

- 110/18 needle

- 8" machine embroidery hoop

- One spool each of Burmilana #12 thread in three flower colors and three leaf colors

- Darning presser foot

HOW TO

1. Transfer the mum pattern at the back of this chapter to the heavy weight fabric, making sure to double the pattern in size. Use any method discussed in Chapter Four to enlarge and transfer the design.

2. Since the leaves are larger than the flower petals it will be easiest to start with the leaves. Follow the same directions as in the practice leaf above.

3. When you are finished with the leaves, set your sewing machine to a 4mm wide zigzag. Stitch five stitches in place in the center of the flower. Leave the needle in the fabric and rotate the hoop to a different spot. Repeat until the center is filled.

4. Next, do the flower petals, following the same directions as in the practice petal above.

5. Embroider the stems with free motion straight stitch starting from the base of the flower and moving up.

6. Sign and date your work with free motion straight stitch following the lettering you have scribed using a water-removable pen.

7. When the embroidery is finished press it wrong side up with a steam iron over a towel, from the wrong side.

Glads in Fill-in Stitch
(see color section)

 THE USE OF RAYON THREAD ADDS SHINE AND LIGHT REFLECTION. This embroidery has five colors in the pink to orange range plus three greens, but because of the added light reflection, the eye tells you there are many more colors. Look for attractive gladiola patterns in seed catalogs and flower books, which are a big help when it comes to stitching realistic natural plant material. Of course, if you can go out in your garden and cut a glad and set it near your sewing machine while you stitch all the better! Or, create a pattern by photocopying the photo in the color section at 165%. Before transferring the pattern to the fabric, mix some fabric paint so that it is very watery and stroke green where you will later stitch the leaves and peach where the blossoms will later be stitched. If you try this, do not be concerned about the paint staying within the line of the design. Painting the fabric beforehand makes it harder to see a few stray stitches. Consequently, it is very forgiving for one of your first pieces of free motion zigzag embroidery. You will need to press the fabric to set the paint so that when the embroidery is washed the paint will not run.

HOW TO

1. Transfer your glad design to the fabric using carbon paper (refer back to Chapter Four for transferring instructions). Set the carbon paper design by ironing it with a hot iron.

2. Thread needle and bobbin in a color appropriate for the outside edge of the petals.

3. Decrease top tension by two numbers.

4. Attach the darning foot.

5. Set sewing machine on 3.5mm zigzag.

6. Lower the feed dogs.

7. Hoop the fabric and stabilizer.

8. Lower the presser foot lever. Take a single stitch and bring the bobbin thread to the surface.

9. Starting on the outside edge of any flower petal, zigzag radiating rows of stitching, making sure to move the fabric left to right and right to left along the petal edge.

10. Change thread color and start at the tips of the last row of stitching, again radiating outward toward the center of the petal. As you stitch in the direction of the center of the flower petal continue varying the stitch length. By stitching beyond the tips of the stitches in the last row the thread colors blend and contribute to the lifelike appearance of the flower. Refer to the color photograph in the color section to see how the colors gradually change.

11. Repeat this with as many colors as possible until you reach the base of the petal next to the flower center.

12. Complete the other petals in this manner. Remember there is no right or wrong placement of color. Color placement is in the eyes of the beholder, and it will appear to change under the influence of light reflecting onto the petal. Is the light coming from the right, the left, or is it splashing down directly from above? You will find the easiest light source to be from above. This is how the glad in the photograph was embroidered.

13. When the entire flower is embroidered, use the straight stitch to outline each petal in the darkest value thread.

14. Beginning at the tip of the leaf, stitch one side first in free motion zigzag with a random jagged stitch slanted toward the center vein and ending at the base of the leaf. Repeat on the other side of the leaf. Use all three leaf colors with varying length stitches. Change thread color as needed to obtain a natural blending of color. If the outside edge of the leaf is not smooth, rethread with the edge color and stitch over it a second time.

15. Remember to decide where the source of light and the shadows will be and to embroider those areas lighter and darker, respectively.

16. Lastly, embroider the stamens of the flower. With a water- or air-soluble pen, draw three lines radiating from the center of the flower. Straight stitch the three lines using a light color rayon thread. At the outer end of each of these lines switch the machine to 3.5mm wide zigzag and sew five to seven stitches in place. This creates a blob and looks very much like the stamen of a real flower.

Supplies

- Fabric paint in flower and leaf colors
- Paint brush
- 40 wt rayon machine embroidery thread in at least four flower colors and three leaf colors
- Machine embroidery bobbin thread
- 100/16 new needle
- Medium weight 8" x 10" white 100% cotton fabric (all-cotton fabric will pucker less)
- 8" x 10" medium weight stabilizer
- Water-soluble pen
- Darning presser foot
- 8" machine embroidery hoop
- Photocopy of glad design
- Sheet of one-time carbon paper
- Water- or air-soluble pen

Maribella in All Her Glory
(see color section)

MARIBELLA HAS A PERSONALITY ALL HER OWN, SO DON'T BE SURPRISED IF SHE MEOWS AT YOU WHEN YOU HAVE FINISHED BRINGING HER TO LIFE!

Portrait embroidery is a combination of straight and zigzag stitches in the free motion mode. To make Maribella's portrait as lifelike as possible, study the direction of the stitches in the color photograph in the color section. Some stitches make straight lines while others radiate or are jagged. Stitch in the direction that the fur lies! Because her eyes and nose are the most critical, they will be stitched last, when you have gained the most confidence. Expect to do several practice pieces before completing a lifelike replica.

Supplies

• 40 wt Madeira rayon article #9842 on 210 yard spools in the following colors: #1059 darkest brown, #1057 dark brown, #1126 medium brown, #1055 champagne, #1001 white, #1087 light gray, #1169 olive green, and #1025 gold

• A photocopy of the color photo of Maribella in the color section of the book (make sure that you have good contrast and that you are able to see the stitched details clearly); cut Maribella's photocopy along the outside edge.

• 90/14 needle

• One spool of white machine embroidery bobbin thread

• 8" x 10" piece of each of white nylon organdy, medium weight cotton/polyester cream color fabric, and medium weight stabilizer

• Darning presser foot

• 6" machine embroidery hoop

HOW TO

1. Thread a 110/18 needle with Madeira 40 wt rayon color #1059 and thread the bobbin with white machine embroidery bobbin thread.

2. Lower the feed dogs, attach the darning presser foot, and decrease the needle tension by one to two numbers. Set the stitch width and length at zero. The bobbin tension remains normal.

3. Place the stabilizer on a table, and then cover it with the cream color fabric. Center the cut-out photocopy paper pattern on top of the fabric. The fabric should be right side up. Finally, center the nylon organdy on top. Place all four layers in the hoop so that the entire picture of Maribella can be seen. Hoop as tight as possible, making sure there are no puckers.

4. Lower the presser foot. Take one stitch and bring the bobbin thread to the surface. Outline all of Maribella's features, including ears, nose, chin, dark furrows of fur, and the fur around the eyes, in straight stitches with darkest brown color #1059 (Fig. 6.28).

6.28 Use straight and zigzag stitches to outline all of Maribella's features in color #1059.

Remember to glance at the color photo of Maribella frequently while stitching. Change machine to 3.5mm wide zigzag. With this widened zigzag add additional thread in the darkest areas of the photocopy. Be sure to use the zigzag stitch from side to side as this will create a heavy line.

5. Change back to straight stitch and thread the machine with dark brown color #1057. Straight stitch all the areas with this color, particularly the brow and cheek area (Fig. 6.29). Switch to zigzag 3.5mm wide and side stitch the darkest areas as seen in the photograph and on the high contrast areas of the photocopy pattern. Blend both the straight and the zigzag stitches into the previous stitches. This is very important when creating lifelike portraits.

6.30 Straight and zigzag stitch the mid-brow, the left side of the head, and the front below the chin using medium brown color #1126.

6.29 Straight stitch all of the previously stitched areas with dark brown color #1057.

6. Change to medium brown color #1126, an important highlight color. Straight stitch the mid-brow, left side of head, and front below the chin (Fig. 6.30). Do not fill in the entire area since other colors of thread will fill in the open spaces. Switch to zigzag stitch where heavy areas of stitching are needed.

7. Change to champagne color #1055 and straight stitch on the lower brow, left cheek, and front (Fig. 6.31). Decrease the importance of the dark brown thread on the lip by overstitching with champagne color.

6.31 Straight stitch the lower brow, the left cheek, the lip, and the front with champagne color #1055.

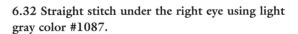

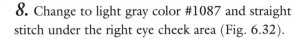

6.32 Straight stitch under the right eye using light gray color #1087.

6.33 Straight stitch both ears, the bridge of the nose, under both eyes, the left cheek, and the front with white color #1001.

8. Change to light gray color #1087 and straight stitch under the right eye cheek area (Fig. 6.32).

9. Change to white color #1001 and straight stitch both ears, the bridge of the nose, under both eyes, left cheek, and front (Fig. 6.33).

10. Rethread with the darkest brown color #1059, stitch the pupil of the eye, and the edges of the nose. Overstitch areas that may have been stitched in with too light a color.

11. Change to olive green color #1169 and straight stitch the eye color around the pupil.

12. Change to gold color #1025 and add just a few straight stitches on either side of the pupil to highlight it. Follow color photographs to embroider the eyes.

13. Change to medium brown color #1126 and straight stitch the nose.

14. Change to champagne color #1055 and switch to zigzag 2mm wide to stitch whiskers radiating from either side of the nose. They should be stitched in satin stitch, while moving the fabric away from you. Refer to the color photograph.

15. To finish, remove from hoop and cut away organdy. Rehoop and add irregular zigzag stitches around the outside edge in several colors to blend the stitching to the fabric. Frame the portrait or make it a pillow and enjoy.

You are a pro!
Now turn to Chapter Seven: Built-in Machine Patterns to make exciting projects featuring pre-programmed patterns.

Hearts to Give
pattern

Sequin Waste Christmas Card pattern

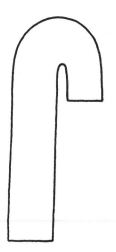

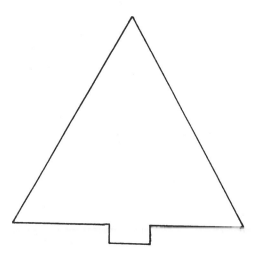

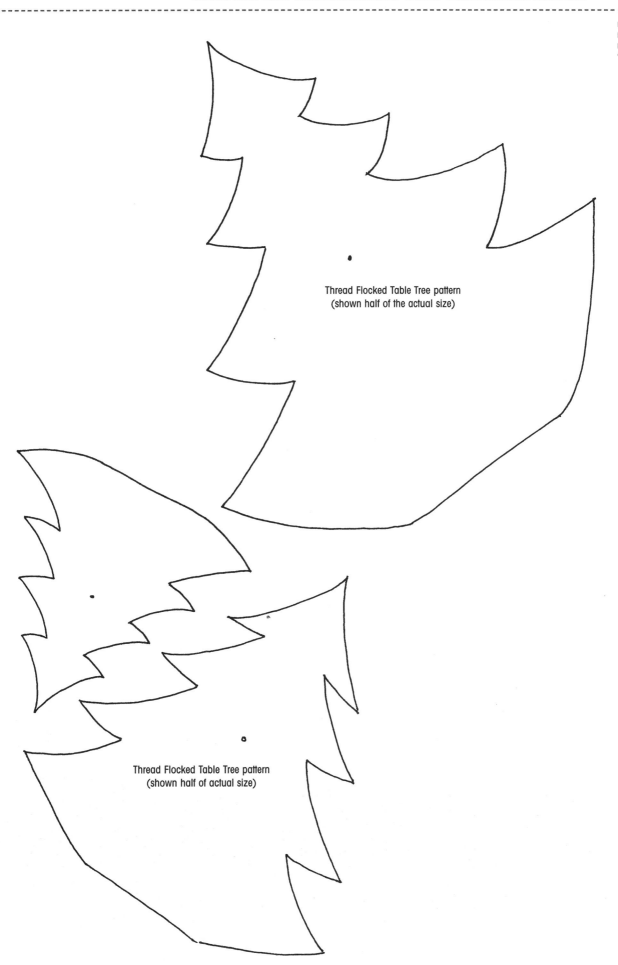

Thread Flocked Table Tree pattern
(shown half of the actual size)

Thread Flocked Table Tree pattern
(shown half of actual size)

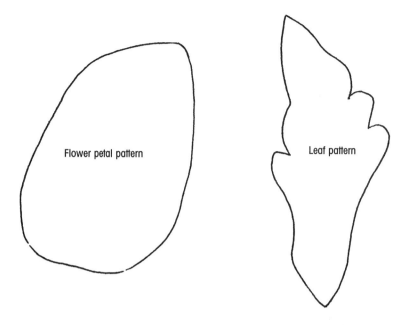

Flower petal pattern

Leaf pattern

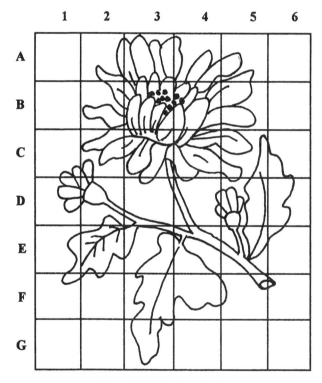

Pattern for Machine Crewelled Mums
(shown half of actual size)

7 Chapter Seven

Built-in Machine Patterns

Using Pre-programmed Patterns in Imaginative Ways

*The harder you work
the luckier you get.*
—Gary Player, golfer

Top of the line sewing machines today have several hundred designs pre-programmed and ready to stitch at the flip of a dial or the push of a button. In this chapter we will explore creative uses of these stitches.

MANIPULATING BUILT-IN STITCHES

Many machines allow the machine embroiderer to elongate the pattern without changing the stitch density (Fig. 7.1). Try increasing the stitch length of a pattern and examine the pattern. Are the stitches as dense as they were prior to increasing the stitch length? This feature gives you a lot of versatility with all pre-programmed stitches and maintains the fine quality of the stitch.

7.1 Elongated stitches should retain the appropriate stitch density.

Fancy Blouse Yoke

 YOU CAN EMBELLISH THE YOKE OF ANY BLOUSE USING PRE-PROGRAMMED STITCHES OF YOUR OWN CHOOSING. Find a blouse in your closet that needs sprucing up or would look great with a particular skirt or pants if it had some embroidery. Or sew a blouse using a medium weight solid color fabric. The only requirement is that it have a yoke.

Because yokes vary greatly, you may enjoy looking through a pattern book for ideas. On the blouse pictured I have offset the embroidered yoke design with Madeira rayon color #2141.

This is an excellent first project using the wonderful stitches of your machine. It will not take you long to look like a professional embroiderer.

7.2 Fancy Blouse Yoke.

Supplies

- Ready-made blouse or blouse pattern

- Fabric for the blouse pattern or, if embroidering the yoke on a ready-made blouse, matching or contrasting fabric 1" larger on all four sides than the ready-made yoke

- 40 wt rayon variegated machine embroidery thread

- Machine embroidery bobbin thread

- New 90/14 needle

- Open toe embroidery foot

- Enough medium weight tear away stabilizer for two layers for all embroidery

- Ruler and water- or air-fade pen or fabric chalk

- Construction thread to match fabric

HOW TO

1. If using a pattern and fabric, cut the yoke pieces 1" larger on all four sides.

Hints

Keep in mind that sewing on the vertical grain of the fabric always produces a smoother embroidery.

It is wise to remove the selvage edge of fabric before beginning to embroider because the selvage is more tightly woven and often causes puckers.

2. Place stabilizer under fabric and pin through fabric and stabilizer from the right side.

3. Decrease top needle tension by one number.

4. Insert new needle and attach the open toe embroidery foot. Thread needle with rayon thread and bobbin with machine embroidery bobbin thread.

5. On the right side of the yoke fabric as you are wearing the blouse, draw a vertical chalk line 1" from the right hand edge of the fabric (Fig. 7.3).

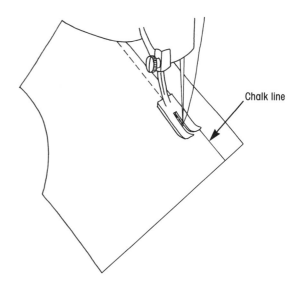

Chalk line

7.3 Sew the first row of stitching with the right edge of the presser foot along the chalk line.

6. If your machine has a sew slow feature and needle down position engage both. If you have none, sew slowly so that the rows of stitching are straight.

7. Use the edge of the presser foot as a guide along the drawn line.

8. Choose seven pre-programmed stitches that are similar. The sample uses menu E1 on the Bernina 1630. All are angular geometric stitches that have both straight stitch and satin stitch in each pattern. Even if your machine only does zigzag and straight stitch you can successfully create this embroidery. For example, stitch four rows of straight stitch ⅛" apart, then stitch three rows of zigzag ¼" apart.

Hint

You will need to press the embroidery frequently, after the first row of stitching and every third row or so.

9. Stitch the first row of stitching on the chalk line. Change to your second stitch selection and sew the second row with the right edge of the presser foot along the left edge of the first row of stitching. Continue changing patterns after every row until all seven patterns have been sewn. Repeat the first pattern and so on until the yoke fabric is completely embroidered. Embroider the left side of yoke in the same manner. If the blouse has a back yoke you may want to embroider it as well.

10. Remove tear away stabilizer and press.

11. If you are making a blouse continue construction, inserting the yokes as directed. If you are embellishing an existing blouse, turn the edges under on all sides to fit the yoke, trim to ½" seam allowance, press, and pin in place. Straight stitch yoke in place with construction thread to match fabric color.

12. Remove pins and press.

Festive Table Frock

 THIS PROJECT USES THE NEEDLE DOWN POSITION AND THE QUILTING BAR TO PRODUCE EVEN ROWS OF BUILT-IN MACHINE PATTERNS ON A TABLE RUNNER, NAPKINS, AND NAPKIN RINGS. If you have a computer assisted machine that allows you to develop your own patterns you may want to use your own designs to create these embellished table runners. Several pre-programmed patterns from the Singer CXL and Pfaff Creative 7550 sewing machines were used in the table setting pictured below.

7.4 **Festive Table Frock.**

TABLE RUNNER HOW TO

1. Decrease needle tension by one number. Insert new 100/16 needle. Attach the embroidery foot and quilting bar. Thread bobbin with machine embroidery bobbin thread. Thread needle with rayon or metallic thread. Engage the needle down position.

2. On a scrap of fabric with two layers of stabilizer underneath, devise a design of patterns using the machine's patterns or those you have developed yourself (Fig. 7.5). The repeat of the pattern should occur every 2" to 3".

7.5 Examples of machine patterns that can be used to embellish the Festive Table Frock.

Supplies

• Striped or solid medium weight, even weave, 18" wide fabric (if you want to line the runner and the scarves purchase double the fabric needed for each)

Table runner: Fabric the length of the table plus 25" (if you want to make a runner that goes across the table, choose fabric the width of the table plus 25")

Napkin rings: Two pieces of 4" x 6" fabric for each napkin ring

Napkins: One piece of 18" x 18" fabric for each napkin

• Two layers of medium weight tear away stabilizer the same dimensions as the fabric for the runner and napkin ring (no stabilizer is necessary for the napkin)

• 40 wt machine embroidery thread in two colors (either metallic or rayon or a combination of both); use a 1000mm spool of the primary color and two to three 200 yard spools of the second color

• Thread stand

• 1000mm machine embroidery bobbin thread

• Quilting bar

• New 100/16 machine needle

• For tassel: A hand sewing needle and cardboard 4" long or an audio cassette

• Construction thread color to match fabric

• Embroidery presser foot

• Hot glue gun and glue

Hints

Since you will be doing yards of top speed sewing, use the thread stand for the needle thread to ensure that the thread runs easily (see Chapter Two).

Occasionally the needle thread will break mid-row in the middle of a pattern. Here is an easy way to resume stitching while making sure the break is never noticed.

1. Push the pattern start or begin button.

2. Note where the pattern begins on the stitch syllabus that comes with your machine.

3. Put the needle in the fabric at that place in the last completely sewn pattern.

4. Adjust the fabric to be sure the presser foot is in good alignment with the previous rows of stitching.

5. Lower the presser foot.

6. Begin stitching slowly. The few stitches stitched over the pattern will not show.

7. Clip threads close to embroidery.

3. After developing a suitable design, ready the runner fabric by putting two layers of stabilizer under it and pin them in place. If the fabric is a solid color, draw a chalk line 1" from the right hand edge.

4. Begin sewing the first row at the top right along the chalk line if the fabric is solid or along a stripe if the fabric is striped. Sew each succeeding row of your design by moving from right to left. This will decrease the possibility of puckers between rows. Repeat the design across the fabric.

Hint

As you approach the half-way mark the fabric will begin running into the machine. Roll the fabric that is hitting the machine jelly roll fashion (Fig. 7.6). Make sure there is a clear space behind the machine for the fabric as you stitch each row.

7.6 When you are machine embroidering large pieces of fabric, roll the fabric up jelly roll style as you go.

5. After all rows have been stitched (the model in the photograph has twenty-eight rows of stitching), press the embroidery on both the right side and the wrong side.

FINISHING

1. If you are not lining the runner fold and press both long edges under ½". Fill the bobbin and the needle with the predominating thread and set sewing machine to 3mm wide zigzag. Stitch length should be set for a satin stitch, .35mm wide. Stitch both long edges, forming a rolled edge look, by zigging on to the material and zagging just off the edge (Fig. 7.7).

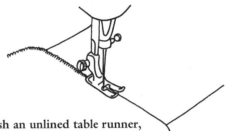

7.7 To finish an unlined table runner, stitch both long edges using a 3mm wide zigzag stitch, being careful to zig onto the material and zag just off the edge.

2. If you wish to line the runner, cut a second piece of fabric the same length and width as the runner or scarf. Pin the two pieces of fabric right sides together. Stitch each long side together with a ½" seam allowance. Turn right side out and press. Then satin stitch edge as in step #1.

3. Fold a short edge in half right sides together and stitch with a ½" seam allowance. Clip point and turn right side out and press as pictured (Fig. 7.8). Repeat on opposite end.

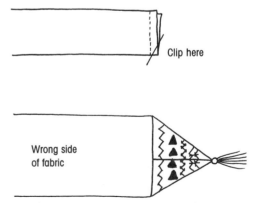

Clip here

Wrong side of fabric

7.8 Fold a short edge in half right sides together and stitch with a ½" seam allowance. Clip the point, turn right side out and press. Repeat on the opposite end.

4. Make a 4" tassel and attach to each point (see below).

SEVEN EASY STEPS TO MAKING YOUR OWN TASSELS

1. Decide on the length of the tassel. An audio-cassette makes a good base. You may also use a credit card or piece of mat or cardboard.

2. Form the hanger by cutting a 15" length of thread from the same spool of thread used in the embroidery. Fold the 15" thread in half and knot the ends together. Lay this on the base you are using to make the tassel.

3. Next, wrap the same color thread from the spool around the base sixty or more times. Remember that the amount of thread seen on one side of the base is only half the size of the finished tassel.

4. Bring the looped end of the hanger through the knotted end, pull tight, and form a knot at top of tassel.

5. Put scissors between the base and thread and cut through all of the tassel threads at the end opposite the hanger (Fig. 7.9).

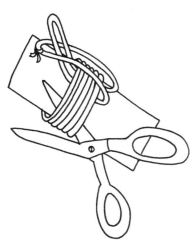

7.9 Put scissors between the base and thread and cut through all of the tassel threads at the end opposite the hanger.

6. Cut a piece of thread 20" long and fold it in half. Use the thread to tie a knot around the tassel threads ½" to 1" below the first knot. This forms the head of the tassel. Then wind the thread ten to fifteen times around the tassel. Thread both ends into a needle and pull up and then down through the wrapped threads (Fig. 7.10). Do this twice, ending by pulling the needle down. Remove the needle.

7.10 Wind the thread ten to fifteen times around the tassel. Thread both ends into a needle and pull up and then down through the wrapped threads.

7. Trim ends, even including the ends of the wrapped thread.

NAPKIN RING HOW TO

These napkin rings are embellished with the same stitch patterns used on the table runner.

1. Stabilize 4" x 6" fabric by putting two layers of stabilizer underneath.

2. In the center of the 4" x 6" fabric, sew one complete pattern of the design sewn on the runner.

3. Line the napkin ring as you did the runner in step #2 under Finishing, above.

4. Turn short edges inside ¼" and straight stitch in place. Finish edges as in step #1 under Finishing, above.

5. Hot glue short edges together.

NAPKIN HOW TO

Several rows of decorative stitching hold the folded edges and mitered corners of the napkin in place.

1. Fold and press under ½" all edges of the 18" x 18" fabric, wrong sides together.

2. Fold all edges under again 1½" (Fig. 7.11a). Open the 1½" fold and fold each corner in as pictured (Fig. 7.11b). Refold on the 1½" line. Straight stitch in place (Fig. 7.11c).

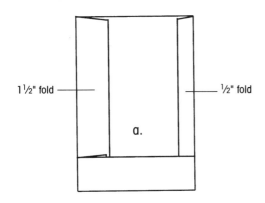

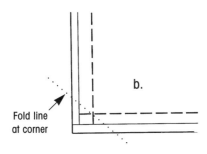

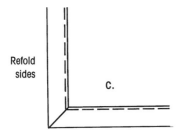

7.11 Fold all edges under again 1½" (a), open the 1½" fold and fold each corner (b), and refold on the 1½" line and straight stitch in place (c).

3. Add two rows of decorative stitching just inside the seam. Choose patterns used in the table runner and napkin rings.

4. Press.

Hint
This is a nice napkin fold for the napkin rings. Pleat the fabric lengthwise (Fig. 7.12a), fold in half (Fig. 7.12b), and insert into the napkin ring (Fig. 7.12c).

7.12 Pleat the fabric lengthwise (a), fold the pleated fabric in half (b), and insert the folded and pleated fabric into the napkin ring (c).

Spectacular Purse
(see color section)

 TO MAKE THIS PURSE, LOOK FOR COLORFUL FABRICS ON THE WHITE ELEPHANT TABLE AT YOUR LOCAL SEWING SUPPLY STORE. Some of the fabrics that work best are fabrics that make you ask yourself "Who would ever wear that?"

This purse utilizes a variety of techniques, including pre-programmed stitches, mirror imaging, needle down, and the twin or triple needle features on your sewing machine. Ribbons and braid on this striking purse are attached to the bold print fabric with the use of these special sewing machine features. Then a surprise finishing touch draws the design together and makes a coherent piece of embroidery.

7.13 Lay ribbons and braids over the fabric, forming a plaid by weaving the ribbons and braids in and out.

Supplies

- Purse pattern

- Purse frames (the frames in the models in the color photo in the color section are from Ghee's Handbag Component Collection; see Source List)

- Bold print fabric the size required by the purse pattern

- Three to four yards each of ribbon, velvet, grosgrain, satin, and metallic braid, in varying widths and lengths

- 40 wt machine embroidery thread in rayon and/or metallic

- Two pieces of medium weight stabilizer the size of the bold print fabric

- One spool of machine embroidery bobbin thread in white or black, whichever blends best with the print fabric

- New 100/16 needle

- Lining fabric as required by purse pattern

HOW TO

1. Thread machine with rayon or metallic embroidery thread.

2. Place two layers of stabilizer the size of the print fabric on a table.

3. Lay fabric over stabilizer right side up.

4. Lay ribbons and braids over the fabric, forming a plaid by weaving in and out (Fig. 7.13). Pin each intersection in place. It is best to use regular dress-making pins because quilting pins are much too long. When all the pins are in place the fabric will feel like a porcupine.

5. Roll fabric so that it easily fits on the bed of the sewing machine. Be cautious of the pins.

6. Select pre-programmed stitches and sew the ribbons and braids in place. You may want to completely cover some ribbons and braids with decorative stitches while leaving others only partially covered.

7. Remove pins and press embroidery after all rows of ribbon have been attached.

8. Set sewing machine to a pre-programmed open stitch and stitch over all of the fabric by abutting rows of stitching in one direction only.

9. Press finished embellished fabric and construct your "Spectacular Purse" from purse pattern.

Hint

Here are some ideas to keep in mind as you embroider the ribbons and braids.

• Try to keep the ribbons straight as you stitch by adjusting them frequently.

• Keep in mind that this is an excellent opportunity to use some of the programmed stitches that you seldom use.

• Try mirror imaging some of the patterns.

• Grosgrain ribbon is very tightly woven and tends to distort when dense embroidery is applied. Do not worry about this because when the final stitches are applied and your embroidery is pressed it will be beautiful.

Patterns in Fours

 CREATING FOUR-SIDED DESIGNS WITH PRE-PROGRAMMED STITCHES IS FUN AND EASY. Even the simplest stitches—overcast and blind hem stitches, for example—make lovely snowflake-like designs. The more complicated stitches with forward and reverse stitching also work well in this mode. Even if you only have utility stitches (mending, hemming, stretch, and overcasting) built into your machine you can be successful at this striking technique. After completing this exercise, place it in a clear plastic page for future reference.

Hint

If your machine has the needle down position, single pattern, and pattern begin (or start), do use them as they will make four-sided patterns easy. If not, hints will be given to assist you. It is fun to make a sampler using most of the stitches pre-programmed into your machine. If your machine allows you to create your own patterns, do so. The large/directional pre-programmed geometric patterns look terrific when using this technique.

7.14 Patterns in Fours Sampler.

Supplies

- 40 wt rayon or metallic machine embroidery thread
- Machine embroidery bobbin thread
- Two layers of heavy stabilizer
- New 90/14 needle
- 8" x 10" medium weight solid color fabric
- Hand sewing needle
- Embroidery presser foot

HOW TO

1. Thread machine with rayon or metallic machine embroidery thread.

2. Lay fabric right side up on top of the stabilizer and place both layers on the bed of the machine with the stabilizer underneath.

3. Select any pattern.

4. Engage the pattern start, single pattern, and needle down features.

Hints

If you don't have the pattern start, single pattern, or needle down features, follow these suggestions.

- If you do not have the pattern start feature, turn the machine off and then on again to automatically start the pattern at the beginning.
- Another way to start a pattern at the beginning is to switch to a different pattern and then switch back to the pattern you wish to stitch.
- If you do not have the needle down feature you will need to use the hand wheel to move the needle down into the fabric before turning the fabric.

5. Stitch one complete pattern and with the needle down, turn the fabric so that it is at a right angle to the pattern stitched. Stitch another complete pattern and with the needle down, turn the fabric another 90°. Repeat this sequence twice more to complete one "pattern in fours."

Hints

You will notice that I did not mention which way to turn the embroidery—to the right or to the left—after the first pattern is complete. You may do either, as long as you are consistent. The completed design will look very different depending on which direction you have moved the fabric. Some patterns will overstitch on the previous pattern when turned in a certain direction. You will need to decide if this is good creative design or not.

A hint that has helped me to line up the presser foot for the second, third, and fourth patterns is to make sure that the presser foot lines up with the direction of the previous pattern threads.

6. Remove the embroidered fabric from the machine. Thread the beginning thread into a hand needle and bring the thread end to the back of the fabric. Repeat with ending thread. Clip ends about 3" from fabric or tie if the embroidery will receive rough wear.

PRINTED FABRIC EMBELLISHED WITH PRE-PROGRAMMED PATTERNS

You will see fabric in a new way as you begin to explore programmed patterns that can embellish some rather bland-looking fabrics. Using a single pattern and repeating that pattern, either randomly or regularly depending on the print, changes fabric dramatically.

7.15 Printed fabric embellished with pre-programmed patterns.

I used some of this type of embellished fabric to make the eyeglass case in the photo using Ghee's Eyeglass frames for the opening (see Source List). The squares were formed by using a manually programmed 5mm wide and 0.3mm long zigzag stitch. I programmed the machine to stitch nine stitches in a row, then stop and tie off. Using the single pattern button I could then stitch random blocks of stitches, which formed little squares.

This exercise allows you to try many different fabrics with various patterns. Look through your stash of fabric or bring a copy of all the machine's patterns with you to the fabric store. Look for

Hint

Consider the following fabric possibilities.

• A fabric that has little squares or rectangles can be reproduced by the use of a zigzag stitch with the stitches touching each other. This is called a satin stitch.

• A small flower pattern can be mimicked with any flower pattern on your machine.

• Find small hearts printed on fabric and embellish some of the hearts with the heart satin stitch pattern built into your machine. For variety try various colors of thread such as red, orange, and pink to stitch the hearts. Shamrocks, bells, ducks, alligators, letters, zodiac signs, trees and leaves, boats, airplanes, and penguins only scratch the surface of the patterns available in today's machines and fabrics.

• Try using geometric patterns placed randomly on plaid or stripe fabric. Squares, circles, diamonds, triangles, and shells are good examples.

• Choose solid color fabric and use a geometric shape to repeat. One of the samples uses the eyelet pattern. For variety, try repeating the eyelet pattern in various sizes in a pot luck fashion over the fabric. Also consider changing the size of the pattern by changing the stitch width. After each single pattern is stitched you may move to another spot and begin another pattern. The thread that is carried from one pattern to another becomes an integral part of the design. A multi-colored thread is a fun choice here.

fabric that has a pattern similar to or exactly opposite of one of your pre-programmed stitches.

AN EXERCISE IN USING PRE-PROGRAMMED PATTERNS (see color section)

You will find that these stitches make useful reference pieces, so add them to your growing number of clear plastic pages.

Supplies

- Machine embroidery presser foot

- Small amount of 40 wt machine embroidery thread in solid, multi-color, or metallic

- Small amount of machine embroidery bobbin thread

- 8" x 10" pieces of medium weight print and/or solid fabric

- Medium weight stabilizer the size of the fabric

- New 90/14 needle

HOW TO

1. Review all the patterns your machine offers.

2. Engage the single pattern button. When you begin sewing, this feature will cause the machine to stitch a single pattern and then stop and tie off the thread. Then you will need to raise the presser foot and move to the next spot you have chosen. Your machine will continue to stitch a single pattern and tie off as long as the single pattern button is engaged.

3. Thread the machine and change to the new 90/14 needle.

4. Place the fabric right side up on top of the stabilizer.

5. Begin stitching using the patterns you have selected. Stitch the pattern or patterns selected in the appropriate places to make a good design.

DOUBLE/TWIN NEEDLE EMBROIDERY

You will hardly believe the transformation in design and color when double needles are threaded with different colors of thread and programmed stitches are stitched. If you wish to stitch a design for a baby, for example, and have no variegated thread, just use the double needle and thread one needle with pink and the other with light blue. Select any pattern and voila! You'll have an instant two-color design.

Double/Twin Needle Bookmark

(see color section)

 A SIMPLE TRIBUTE TO TWIN NEEDLE EMBROIDERY, THIS BOOK-MARK IS EASY AND FUN TO MAKE.

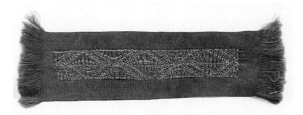

7.16 Double/Twin Needle Bookmark.

Supplies

- 6"x 4" piece of medium weight fabric

- 1½" x 5" piece of medium weight stabilizer

- 30 wt metallic and rayon machine embroidery threads in colors to coordinate with fabric

- Machine embroidery bobbin thread

- 2.0/80 twin needle

- Embroidery presser foot

HOW TO

1. Follow the instructions in your sewing machine manual to insert a new twin needle and thread the machine. On most machines, you will need to thread each thread on either side of the tension disk. Some machines have a dual guide just above the needle to aid in threading. After threading the guide or guides, thread each needle and bring both threads under the presser foot and to the back of the machine as you usually do. Bring the machine embroidery bobbin thread from the case through the throat plate and to the back of the machine.

2. Decrease needle tension one number, attach embroidery presser foot, and engage the twin needle guarded width.

3. With fabric right side up, center stabilizer under fabric.

4. Select a pre-programmed stitch that is moderately open.

5. Start stitching the length of the fabric 1" from the top edge and a stitch width from the center. End stitching 1" from edge of fabric.

6. Stitch a second row of the same pattern, abutting the right edge of the first row pattern and ending as before.

7. Fringe both ends of the fabric ½".

8. Fold long edges right sides together, and straight stitch with ½" seam allowance.

9. Turn right side out and press.

Mirror Image Sampler

 ADD THE MIRROR IMAGING FEATURE TO A TWIN NEEDLE DESIGN AND YOU WILL HAVE EVERYONE ASKING, HOW DID YOU DO THAT? It is great fun to fool people with such a simple technique.

The pattern begin feature is invaluable with the mirror imaging technique since it enables you to start the pattern at the very beginning; you may then mimic the pattern already stitched by flipping it over with the mirror image button (Fig. 7.17).

Supplies

- 40 wt rayon or metallic thread
- Machine embroidery bobbin thread
- New 2.0/80 twin needle
- 12" x 12" medium weight solid color fabric
- Two pieces of medium weight stabilizer the same size as the fabric
- Embroidery presser foot
- Chalk and ruler

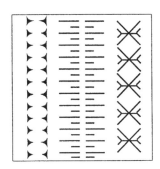

7.17 Patterns sewn with the mirror image feature.

HOW TO

1. Thread the machine as directed by your manual for twin needles.

2. Decrease the needle tension by one number, and engage the twin needle guarded width.

3. Draw a chalk line 1" from the edge of the fabric in the direction the rows of stitching will be stitched.

4. Lay both pieces of stabilizer under fabric.

5. Choose a scallop satin stitch, push the pattern start button, and stitch a single row on the chalk line.

6. Now activate the pattern begin, needle down, and mirror image features of your sewing machine.

7. The scallop stitches will now be reversed. Put the needle in the hole in which the previous row began and stitch another row abutting the previous row.

8. Choose another asymmetrical built-in pattern. Stitch this row of stitching a presser foot away from the first two rows.

9. Stitch the new asymmetrical pattern and repeat steps #6 and #7.

10. Continue choosing asymmetrical built-in

patterns, stitching the first row and then reversing the direction of the pattern with the mirror image feature until the area you want embellished is covered.

Hint

To help both rows of stitching line up perfectly:

• In order for the same stitch length and density to be stitched by the machine it is imperative that there be no obstacles to obstruct the movement of the fabric through the machine. If there is excess material rubbing next to the machine, roll the fabric.

• Remember to only guide the fabric. Do not push or pull the fabric while the stitches are being formed.

• If a thread breaks, rethread your machine and push the pattern begin/start. Reinsert the needle into the first stitch of the last complete pattern. You may be stitching over a few stitches, but the extra stitches will not show.

Your sampler will serve as a reminder of the interesting design possibilities this technique holds.

USING HEAVY THREAD IN THE BOBBIN

The use of heavy thread in the bobbin has always fascinated me. Even straight stitching becomes more dramatic when heavy thread is used in the bobbin. Try some built-in stitches. They will look as though they have been hand couched. (A term used in hand embroidery to mean the attachment of one thread to the surface of fabric by a second thread.) Double needle stitching with this method is not effective since the bobbin thread is what is of interest.

Heavy Thread Sampler

IN ADDITION TO MAKING A SAMPLER FOR YOU TO REFER BACK TO AS YOUR EMBROIDERY EXPERTISE DEVELOPS, YOU CAN USE HEAVY THREADS IN THE BOBBIN TO ADD AN UNUSUAL DECORATIVE TOUCH TO NAPKIN EDGES, BLOUSE FRONTS, TOWELS, MONOGRAMS, AND CHRISTMAS DECORATIONS.

Supplies

• Heavy thread such as crochet cotton, Decor 6, Glamour, Pearl Cotton, cotton embroidery floss, or ribbon floss for the bobbin

• Machine embroidery bobbin thread for the needle

• New 90/14 machine needle

• 8" x 10" medium to heavy weight fabric

• 8" x 10" heavy weight stabilizer

• Regular presser foot

HOW TO

1. Wind the bobbin with the heavy thread either by hand or in the usual way using the sewing machine's bobbin winder.

2. Decrease the bobbin tension about half a turn of the tension screw, loosening the tension until the heavy thread runs through the bobbin easily. Leave the needle tension balanced.

3. Do a test stitch to ensure that the stitches are well formed and that tensions are correct.

4. To begin the actual stitching, place the fabric right side down on the bed of the sewing machine with the stabilizer on top of the fabric. Lower the presser bar. Take one stitch and pull

7.18 A sampler made from heavy thread in the bobbin.

on the needle thread to force the bobbin thread to the surface. Doing this eliminates the possibility that the bobbin thread will become tangled in the embroidery.

Hints

Many sewers do not want to manipulate the tension of the bobbin they use for regular sewing and so they decide to purchase a second bobbin case just for embroidery. Some sewing machine manufacturers make a special embroidery bobbin, which has added space to accommodate heavy threads. Ask your dealer.

Consult your sewing machine manual or your dealer if you are uncertain about changing the bobbin tension. Read about tensions in Chapter One.

The stitch is perfect when there is no distortion or pulling of the bobbin (heavy) thread. If the bobbin tension is too loose the bobbin (heavy) thread will have loops and will not lie flat and secure to the fabric. If the needle tension is too loose it will leave little "spider legs" of the needle thread around the heavy thread. If the needle tension is too tight the stitches will pucker.

When the needle tension is loosened by a couple of numbers it will be seen on the right side of the embroidery crossing over the bobbin thread. This can add another dimension of color or texture to the embroidery. The "spider legs" can also be used to design advantage although I would not suggest using it in an embroidery that will receive a lot of wear.

Try stitching straight stitches first and then select several built-in patterns. The sampler shows several kinds of heavy thread, metallic, wool/ acrylic, and viscose.

Jacket Deluxe!
(see color section)

 HERE IS A JACKET EMBELLISHMENT UTILIZING HEAVY EMBROIDERY THREAD IN THE BOBBIN. CHOOSE A JACKET OR VEST PATTERN WITH SIMPLE LINES—NO COLLAR, CUFFS OR POCKETS. Darts for fitting should originate from the waist only. A lined jacket will hide all of the ends of threads from the embroidery.

HOW TO

1. Cut the jacket and flannel fabric from the pattern, making the fabrics 1" larger than the pattern on all sides. This is to ensure that the jacket and lining fabrics will be large enough after the embroidery is done and to ensure that there is enough fabric to hoop when embroidering near the seam lines.

2. Select the jacket embroidery patterns at the end of this chapter and transfer them to tracing paper, making sure to double in size some of the patterns, as indicated on the patterns themselves

(see instructions for enlarging and transferring designs in Chapter Four).

3. Decide on placement of pattern on jacket front (Fig. 7.19a), back (Fig. 7.19b), and one sleeve (Fig. 7.19c).

4. Thread the bobbin with heavy metallic thread and adjust the bobbin tension so that the heavy thread moves through the bobbin case easily. You may want to refer to "Adjusting Sewing Machine Tensions" in Chapter One.

5. Thread the needle with 40 wt machine embroidery thread to match heavy thread. Decrease needle tension by ½ a number.

Hint

Because a single bobbin won't hold much heavy thread, it is a good idea to fill several bobbins with the heavy thread before you begin embroidering so as to have them ready as you embroider.

Supplies

- Solid color fabric, a ¼ yard more than the pattern suggests

- Regular pre-shrunk cotton flannel fabric double the amount suggested by the pattern

- Lining fabric as indicated by the pattern; "slippery" fabric such as polyester or silk will make it easier to put the jacket on over another garment

- A 100 meter spool of heavy weight metallic or rayon thread (Decor 6 or Glamour) for the jacket embellishment

- One spool of 40 wt rayon or metallic machine embroidery thread for the needle; choose a color to complement the heavy weight thread

- Machine embroidery bobbin thread

- Garment construction thread to match the jacket fabric

- New 100/16 needle to do the embroidery

- New 90/14 needle for the garment construction

- 8" machine embroidery hoop

- Darning presser foot

- Tracing paper

- Hand needle with large enough eye to accommodate heavy thread

- Quilting bar

- Regular presser foot

- Ruler and chalk

6. Attach the darning foot.

7. Put the traced pattern on an outside window or over a light table so that the pattern may be reversed by tracing over the lines on the back side of the embroidery pattern.

8. Lay the outside of the hoop on a table. Place the fashion fabric right side down over the hoop.

Then lay two layers of flannel over the fashion fabric. Next, center the retraced pattern, side A down, as desired. Hoop all four layers so that the fabric is taut and will not flutter up and down during stitching.

9. Put the hoop under the darning foot and **lower the presser bar lever.** Take a single stitch and bring the bobbin thread to the surface.

A. Front

B. Back

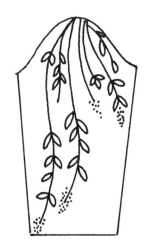

C. Sleeve

7.19 Position the appropriate pattern on the jacket front, back, and sleeve.

10. Using a 2.5mm straight stitch, stitch through the pattern lines. You will find that there are places in the design that must be stitched twice in order to get to the next part of the design. Stitch all of the design that is within the area of the hoop before moving the hoop to the next area.

11. After finishing all of the embroidery, bring the heavy thread ends to the inside of the garment with a hand needle. Tie the threads in a knot or cut them, leaving at least 3".

12. Tear away the tracing paper from the stitching, being careful not to disturb the stitching.

13. Rethread bobbin with the 40 wt machine embroidery thread, which is also in the needle. Readjust the bobbin tension to balanced.

Readjust the needle tension so that it is decreased by one number.

14. Set sewing machine to a 3.0mm straight stitch. Attach the regular presser foot, 90/14 needle and quilting bar. On the fashion fabric of the sleeves, back, and fronts of the jacket, draw vertical chalk lines beginning 1" from the right edge. Sew vertical rows of stitching one inch apart over each of these pattern parts. Use the quilting bar as a guide allowing it to ride on the previous row of stitches. Do not stitch through the embroidery. Instead stitch up to the design only.

15. Use a hand needle to bring all threads to the back of the embroidery.

16. Recut jacket to the size of the pattern and finish as directed in the pattern.

CREATING WITH PRE-PROGRAMMED MANIPULATED STITCHES

Here is a meaningful way to change the programmed stitches built into your machine.

AN EXERCISE USING PRE-PROGRAMMED MANIPULATED STITCHES

Many of the built-in stitches can be changed in width or length or added together with other patterns to make unique designs. What follows are program changes in either the width, length, or density of built-in stitches common to many machines today. You will find that these changes can be incorporated into many designs. Three simple designs are offered for you to re-create.

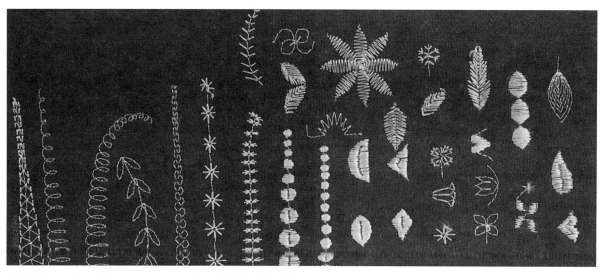

7.20 A sampler of pre-programmed manipulated stitches.

Each of these designs could easily be used on a pocket, pot holder, tea towel, framed, or stitched in several colors to form a quilted wall hanging.

Supplies

- Two pieces of 10" x 10" medium to heavy weight fabric

- Four pieces of 10" x 10" medium weight stabilizer

- 40 wt rayon machine embroidery thread in two flower colors and two leaf colors

- One spool of white machine embroidery bobbin thread

- 90/14 sewing machine needle

HOW TO

1. First begin by reviewing your sewing machine's manual regarding the memory in your machine.

2. Select stitches that may look like branches or flower stems. Loops, honeycombs, stars, and feathers work well, as do zigzags and three step zigzags.

3. Following your machine's directions to store a built-in stitch in memory, enter one or two single patterns then change the stitch width by decreasing it a half or whole number. Put this in memory and continue decreasing the width and adding the pattern to memory until the machine will no longer accept further decreases. Enter each of the stitches in step #2 into a separate memory using this method of manipulation.

4. Using the single pattern button, stitch what you have put in memory. It will look similar to

the stems and branches in Fig. 7.20. Do this for several patterns so that you will have a small repertoire of branches and flower stems to choose from.

5. Review seed catalogs or a flower book and notice the elements, or flowers and leaves. Diamonds, ovals, circles, stars, tear drops, various leaves, scallops, and shells, as well as hearts and eyelets, are just some of the stitches from your machine that will correspond to flower component shapes. Insert these stitches into your machine's memory as per step #3. Remember to use the single pattern key.

6. Make a sampler on heavy fabric and a medium weight stabilizer by using both the altered stitches in memory and all of the stitches from your machine that will be good flower and leaf components. Next form flower heads and branches with leaves using the flower components you have selected. With some of the altered stitch groupings in memory, change the direction by "bending" the branches. Add this sampler to your plastic pages to jog your memory as you create designs.

7. Use the prick and pounce transfer method to transfer one of the designs from the back of the chapter onto the second piece of fabric. Lay two layers of stabilizer under the fabric and place on the bed of the sewing machine. Stitch the lines to resemble branches. Fill in with other branches and flower heads. Add leaves last. Remember, a design is only a plan. Make it your own by adding a branch or two or a flower bud.

Hint

Wall paper patterns are good places to find free flowing designs. Most wall paper stores will give discontinued books away or only ask a nominal fee.

MONOGRAMMING WITH PROGRAMMED STITCHES

A monogram has one or more letters, often interwoven to form a single motif. The alphabets pre-programmed into today's top of the line sewing machines vary in size from ¼" to more than 1". Some are block letters and others are double stitched block letters. There are many variations of script letters as well. Some letters have modest curves, while others have more elaborate swirls that clamor for added embellishment with some of the built-in flower designs. Monogrammed clothing has long been a status symbol and is ultra easy to make using built-in alphabets.

Two and three letter monograms on clothing are commonly located in the following areas.

- **Pockets:** Top left corner or centered.

- **Cuffs:** On the button hole side of the left cuff

beginning ½" from the fold, ¼" from the seam that attaches the cuff to the shirt, or ¼" from the bottom edge of the cuff on the center back (away from the button hole).

- **Pant leg:** ½" from hem, at center seam on outside of left leg.

- **Turtlenecks:** ½" from bottom edge at center front or to the left of center 1½".

Monograms on household items are usually placed in the following locations.

- **Table cloths:** At a corner or the center of any side.

- **Placemats:** On the top left side.

- **Towels:** Between 1" and 2" above the border depending on the size of the towel.

Shirt Pocket Monogram
Plus Large Program Pattern Embellishment

CHANGE A PURCHASED BLOUSE DRAMATICALLY BY USING EITHER THE LARGE/DIRECTIONAL SEWING PATTERNS OR SMALLER PRE-PROGRAMMED PATTERNS COMBINED WITH MONOGRAMS. Explore ways to make the pre-programmed letters intertwine to form graceful motifs. Even if your machine does not have these large patterns, you can embroider the letters using free motion embroidery and at the same time add the swirls and curves that create monogram motifs that look and feel like they belong together.

Monogramming works best if the fabric is of medium weight and even weave. Solids, stripes, and plaids all work well depending on the color thread used. Your options vary a great deal here, too. For a subtle look, choose thread the same shade as the fabric. Or choose a darker or lighter value for a slight contrast. For a bright colorful look, choose a monogram color in high contrast to the fabric. Navy and white fabric embellished with a red monogram is a good example.

Supplies

- A purchased blouse with a pocket that can be removed easily or a pattern for a blouse that will accommodate a pocket on the left front

- Thread, fabric, stabilizer, and other materials as described by the blouse pattern instructions

- Spool of 40 wt rayon thread in the color of your choice

- Embroidery presser foot or follow the manufacturer's suggestion for embroidering large patterns

- New 90/14 needle

- Two layers of very firm stabilizer twice the size of the monogram

- Garment construction thread to match fabric

7.21 Shirt pocket monogram.

7.22 Large program pattern embellishment.

HOW TO

1. Remove pocket from blouse or cut pocket from blouse pattern. Press.

2. Thread needle and bobbin with 40 wt rayon machine embroidery thread.

3. Select your monogram patterns.

4. Decrease needle tension by one number. This will create smoother edges and a smoother top stitch because the needle thread will be brought to the back of the embroidery instead of to the edge of the stitch.

5. Place stabilizer under pocket. Mark placement of monogram. If it is three letters and the last initial will be larger than the other two letters, mark placement of the large letter first and embroider it.

6. Next mark the placement of the first initial and embroider it. Then mark and embroider the third initial.

7. Remove stabilizer from edge of embroidery and press. Be sure to remove all of the old threads from the edge of the pocket and on the blouse where the pocket was previously.

8. Return needle tension to a balanced stitch and attach the regular presser foot.

Thread machine with garment construction thread.

9. Pin pocket to blouse where it was previously sewn and stitch in place using construction thread to match fabric. Press.

Hints

For easy monogramming with large programmed patterns, keep the following points in mind.

• The feed dogs move the fabric from side to side when stitching the large directional pre-programmed letters. You should not try to guide the fabric, but instead, simply let the feed dogs do their work.

• Use stripe or plaid fabric or draw a vertical chalk line on solid fabric. No matter how the presser foot moves across the fabric the edge of the presser foot should always be parallel to the stripe or chalk line.

• Practice, practice, practice. Once the machine is set correctly and the stabilizer is the correct weight to prevent puckering, the rest is up to you. It helps to know where the machine will stitch next. In other words, in what direction will the presser foot move the fabric? Is it stitching, for instance, the bar of the letter in the correct place? Knowing what to expect will save you from ripping.

• It is important that the area to be monogrammed be well pressed. I have found that a couple of squirts of spray starch firms up the material. The spray starch also allows the fabric, and especially the stabilizer, to glide easily over the bed of the sewing machine during the stitching process.

• Stitching large pre-programmed stitches down the front of the blouse turned out to be more of a challenge than I had thought. The blouse I embroidered had a double layer of fabric with a stabilizer in between. I automatically added an additional layer of stabilizer and began to embroider. After several tries of uneven patterns I realized that the stabilizer was creating too much drag, causing the fabric to stay in one place too long, thus creating stitch build-up and an uneven pattern. When I removed the stabilizer altogether the problem was eliminated.

• When embroidering the front facing of a ready-made blouse remember to plan the embroidery so that it does not interfere with the button holes.

• A monogram can be stitched on to a small swatch of fabric and then appliquéd later.

MACHINE PATTERNED FABRIC

When I first discovered this technique I sat at my sewing machine for hours stitching built-in patterns from my sewing machine. The only difference was that now I was abutting each row to the previous row and making a solid tapestry-like fabric. You too will be addicted. The combinations of thread and pattern are fascinating.

Although solid color threads work with this technique, I believe that multi-colored threads are far more effective because they automatically produce color patterns that work across the surface of the design. This creates counter rhythms that add immeasurably to the visual interest. Metallic threads are very effective because the play of reflective light creates movement and dimension in much the same way that changing the colors does.

Using fabric that matches the thread color results in an embossed look. When the fabric matches one of the colors in the multi-color thread, the stitches that are the same color as the fabric will disappear. Of course, the stitches are there, but they disappear even at a short distance and the result is intriguing.

AN EXERCISE IN MAKING MACHINE PATTERNED FABRIC

Supplies

- 40 wt rayon or metallic machine embroidery thread
- 10" x 10" medium weight solid fabric
- Two pieces of medium weight stabilizer the same size as the fabric
- Embroidery presser foot
- New 90/14 needle
- Chalk and a ruler
- Iron

HOW TO

1. Thread machine and bobbin.

2. Insert a new 90/14 needle.

3. Attach the embroidery presser foot.

4. Decrease the needle tension by two numbers.

5. Draw a chalk line 1" from the right edge of the fabric in the direction you'll stitch.

6. Lay stabilizer under the fabric and place the layers with the fabric right side up under the presser foot so that the first row will be stitched on the edge of the chalk line.

7. For your first piece select two patterns, one open and the other a dense satin stitch pattern. Stitch the first row of open stitches on the chalk line. Next select the dense pattern and stitch the second row so that the stitches abut the stitches of the first row. Continue interchanging the two patterns until the fabric is covered with stitching (Fig. 7.23).

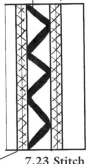

First row of dense satin stitches

Repeat of first row

First row of open stitches.

7.23 Stitch the second row so the stitches abut the first row stitches.

8. Press with a hot steam iron frequently.

Hints

For choosing stitches:

- First select an open pattern such as a honeycomb or a stretch stitch. For the second row of stitches look for patterns that are dense and are predominately satin stitch.
- Another option is the use of a single stitch such as a zigzag stitched in four directions (Fig. 7.24). (See the "Four Way Zigzag Make-up Bag" in Chapter Six.)

7.24 The zigzag stitch stitched in four directions.

- Try stitching the embroidery using one stitch of an open pattern.
- Conversely use a dense satin stitch pattern only.
- Every manufacturer's embroidery presser foot is different so you will need to decide where on the presser foot to watch to ensure that the two rows abut. If the rows do not abut consistently your eye will travel immediately to the place where there's a gap and the rhythm of the embroidery will be spoiled.
- Because the embroidery is dense, the finished piece is a bit stiff. While it won't be suitable for an entire garment, it will make an elegant yoke or purse. You will find many uses for this type of embroidery, including placemats and checkbook covers.

Embroidered Checkbook Cover
(see color section)

 THIS CHECKBOOK COVER EMBELL-ISHED WITH MACHINE PATTERNED STITCHES LOOKS LIKE A PIECE OF TAPESTRY FABRIC. You will be surprised by its durability and easy care, as it can be washed by hand and needs only a light pressing.

HOW TO

1. Sew machine patterned fabric following the general directions earlier in this chapter. The rows of stitching should be stitched vertically over the length of the checkbook.

2. Use chalk to mark the machine patterned fabric the same size as the checkbook plus ½" on each side and 1" at top and bottom. Cut embroidered fabric to this size. Top and bottom should be at the end and beginning of the stitch rows.

3. Sew the two 4" x 7" strips of fabric to the top and bottom of the embroidered fabric with a ½" seam allowance, right sides together (Fig. 7.25).

4. Next, turn top of embroidery right sides together 1" beyond the seam made by attaching the 4" x 7" strip of fabric.

5. Fold raw edge of fabric strip addition under 1", making sure wrong sides are

Supplies

- Solid color fabric 2" wider and 2" longer than the checkbook

- Two layers of stabilizer the same size as the fabric

- Two additional pieces of fabric each measuring 4" x 7"; these make a portion of the inside pocket, which will remain unembellished.

- One spool of multi-color 40 wt machine embroidery thread

- New 90/14 sewing machine needle

- Chalk and ruler

together, and pin. Stitch side ½" from the edge (Fig. 7.26).

6. Repeat steps #4 and #5 on opposite edge.

7. Turn "pockets" right side out and insert checkbook.

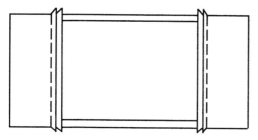

7.25 Using a ½" seam allowance, sew the two 4" x 7" strips of fabric to the top and bottom of the embroidered fabric, right sides together.

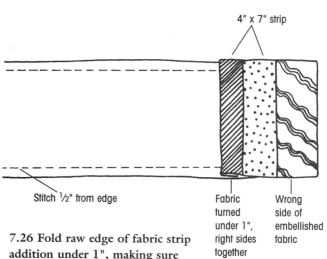

4" x 7" strip

Stitch ½" from edge

Fabric turned under 1", right sides together

Wrong side of embellished fabric

7.26 Fold raw edge of fabric strip addition under 1", making sure wrong sides are together, and pin. Stitch side ½" from edge.

HEAVY THREADS COUCHED WITH PROGRAMMED PATTERNS

In this technique, programmed stitches are sewn over threads laid on the fabric, which allows the combining of two colors of thread. I find it useful especially when combining red and green, two colors not commonly found combined into one machine embroidery thread.

Sampler of Programmed Stitches Over Heavy Threads
(see color section)

 USE THIS PIECE OF EMBROIDERY TO MAKE A SAMPLER FOR YOUR WALL OR AS AN EXERCISE TO BE ADDED TO YOUR CLEAR PLASTIC PAGE NOTEBOOK OF MACHINE EMBROIDERED SAMPLES. Refer to Chapter Three to review the threads most suitable for couching.

Supplies

• A variety of heavy threads such as Decor 6, Glamour, Pearl Cotton, Burmilana, and heavy metallics

• 40 wt rayon or metallic machine embroidery needle thread that complements or contrasts couched threads

• Machine embroidery bobbin thread to match fabric

• 8" x 10" medium to heavy weight fabric

• Two pieces of 8" x 10" stabilizer

• New 100/16 needle

• Cording foot with at least three grooves that are a little larger than the thread to be couched (Fig. 7.28)

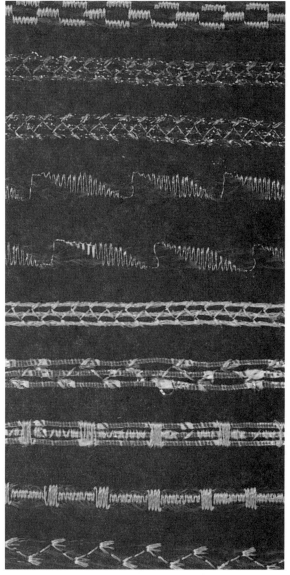

7.27 A sampler of programmed stitches over heavy threads.

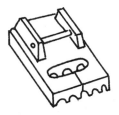

7.28 A cording foot has grooves cut into the underside of the foot.

HOW TO

1. Thread needle and bobbin, decrease top tension by one number, attach cording presser foot and new 100/16 needle.

2. Lay fabric right side up with two layers of stabilizer under it on bed of sewing machine.

3. Cut three strands of heavy thread 2" longer than the length of the fabric to be embellished. Lay the ends of these three threads under the middle grooves of the cording presser foot. Lower presser foot.

4. Select a pre-programmed stitch of moderate density. Some satin stitches and some open or straight stitches within the pattern are ideal.

5. Now simply stitch over the threads. If the grooves of the cording foot are much larger than the thread to be couched you may find that the threads may not stay in the grooves. To prevent this, lay the thread flat and even on the fabric or use a multiple cording guide to keep the heavy threads straight under the correct grove in the cording foot (see Source List).

Chapter Seven concludes the projects in Teach Yourself Machine Embroidery. Now you have the knowledge and skill necessary to design and create your own fabulous projects. I hope that you will find new ways to use your sewing

> ### Hint
> One variation is to program your machine to stitch several different patterns one after another. To do this select a pattern and push the single pattern button. Follow the manufacturer's directions to program your machine. After you have the first single pattern entered in memory choose another pattern and enter it into memory. Repeat this until the desired number of patterns are entered. You may wish to use only two patterns, in which case the machine will alternate between the two patterns.
>
> If your machine has a sew slow feature this is a good time to use it. Remember the sew slow feature only allows you to sew at one third to one half the full speed even though the foot petal is pressed to the maximum.

machine and that you have many, many more hours of creative sewing enjoyment ahead.

In Chapter Eight: When Things Go Wrong, you will find many trouble-shooting suggestions which will help you if you are having technical problems with your sewing machine or thread. A brief read through it may help you avoid some of the most common embellishment difficulties.

Good luck and happy stitching.

Jacket Deluxe! patterns

Jacket Deluxe! pattern

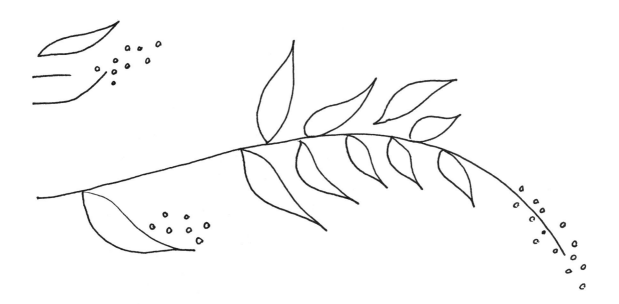

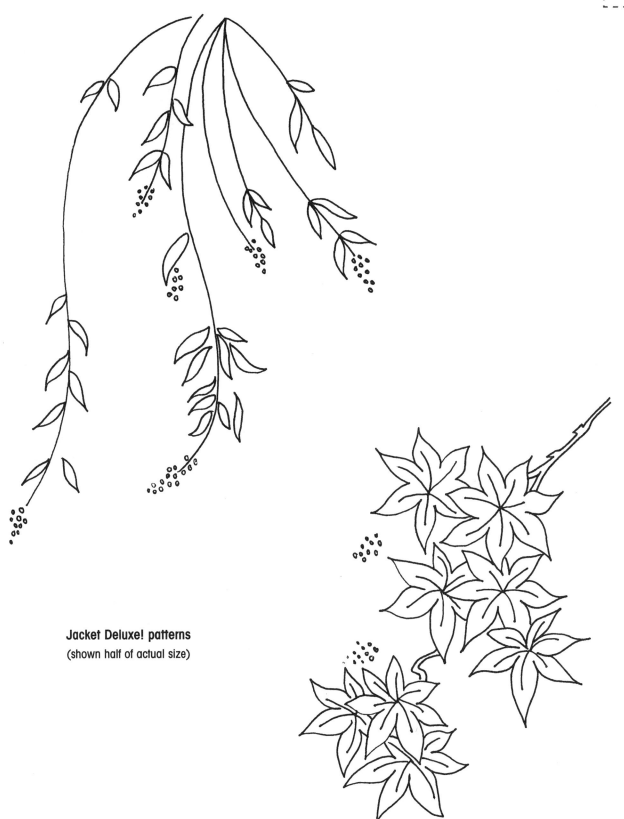

Jacket Deluxe! patterns
(shown half of actual size)

Jacket Deluxe! patterns
(shown half of actual size)

**Pattern for creating
with pre-programmed
manipulated stitches**

**Patterns for creating
with pre-programmed
manipulated stitches**

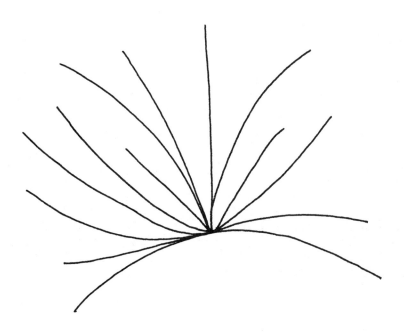

When Things Go Wrong

Common Predicaments in Machine Embroidery and How to Solve Them

> *Accept the challenges, so that you may feel the exhilaration of victory.*
> —General George S. Patton

The more machine embroidery you do the fewer problems you will have since most of the challenges encountered relate to your familiarity with your sewing machine. Completely rethreading your sewing machine, both needle and bobbin, will eliminate 90% of your embroidery challenges. No matter the problem, I always tell my students to rethread their machines. Often, they tell me that they rethreaded their machines just stitches ago. Nevertheless, it is amazing how often rethreading solves the problem. There seems to be a little gnome that rethreads sewing machines after stitching begins! So the moral of the story is that if you are having trouble, rethread the needle and bobbin of the sewing machine.

The second most common error is to begin stitching in the free motion embroidery mode without lowering the presser bar lever. Check the lever! If rethreading your machine fails to eliminate the challenge, then follow the simple suggestions below. But first, to keep machine embroidering fun, please review the following safety instructions.

SAFETY ISSUES TO KEEP IN MIND

- Unplug or turn off the sewing machine when changing a needle or filling the bobbin case.

- Unplug or turn off your sewing machine whenever you clean the bobbin or remove a snarl of thread. Remember that your sewing machine doesn't have a conscience—it will sew through just about anything, even your finger!

- If you are an impatient sewer and turning off or unplugging the machine seems like too much work, at least take your foot completely away from the foot petal.

- When learning machine embroidery use the darning foot until you have mastered the skill of moving the fabric under the needle without it.

- A child using a sewing machine needs supervision and encouragement.

- Oil and clean the machine, especially the bobbin case area, after every four to six hours of machine embroidery. Machine embroidery creates more lint, threads, and dust than regular sewing because the machine commonly runs without stopping for much longer periods of time.

- Have your sewing machine serviced yearly so that it can be thoroughly cleaned, the timing checked, and the programmed stitches rebalanced.

- Review the instructions for "Caring for Your Sewing Machine" in Chapter One.

- When transporting your sewing machine secure it in the trunk. If you must place it on the back seat, be sure to use the seat belt to secure it.

TOP THREAD BREAKS OR SHREDS

This is the most common problem and the one I had the most trouble with when I began machine embroidery.

- The needle needs to be large enough to make a sufficient hole in the fabric to prevent wear of the thread. Try a larger needle or one of the new needles for machine embroidery. See the needle chart in Chapter Three.

- Machine embroidery threads of rayon and metallic tend to be slippery. Threads slip off the spool frequently and wind around the spool holder pin, preventing further thread from running through the tension disks and needle. It is sometimes helpful to compress the ends of thread toward the center of a cop spool. A horizontal spool holder will keep thread from slipping off the spool. Cover spool with mesh or nylon sleeve.

- The needle thread tension may be too tight. Loosen the top tension a little at a time until the thread stops breaking.

- The fabric may not be tight enough in the hoop or it may not be lying flat on the bed of the sewing machine when the stitch is taken. Since the fabric follows the needle up after each stitch the thread wears and breaks.

- If the needle is in backwards or not all the way into the needle holder, the thread will break. Follow directions in your sewing machine manual for removing and inserting a needle.

- If the thread is old it may have dried out. Lack of moisture in thread tends to make it weaker. Leave the spool in the refrigerator or in the bathroom for a day or two to absorb moisture.

- If you are just beginning to do free motion embroidery without a presser foot you may be jerking the fabric, which causes the thread or needle to stretch and break. Go back to using the darning foot until you are a little more comfortable with free motion embroidery.

- Are you using an old needle? A blunt needle will cause thread breakage. Use a new one.

- Metallic threads sometimes knot between the time they leave the spool and when they arrive at the sewing machine needle. Try taping a large eyed hand sewing needle to the back of the sewing machine. Place the thread through the hand needle and then thread the machine in the usual way.

- Begin sewing slowly. A quick start can snap rayon and metallic threads.

- If you are sewing with metallic thread in the needle and it is breaking, change to a larger needle. You can use a 100/16 needle when embroidering with metallic thread.

- Some decorative threads become worn as they go through the last thread guide before the needle. Omit this thread guide and be certain that the rest of the threading path is correct.

- Has the bobbin thread slipped out of its correct threading path in the bobbin case?

- Are you using the recommended bobbin for your sewing machine? Often bobbins seem to fit but do not run smoothly in the bobbin case. Are the edges of the bobbin smooth so that the bobbin can rotate in the case easily?

SKIPPED STITCHES

- The most common reason for skipped stitches is that the fabric is not flat on the bed of the sewing machine at the time the stitch is formed. In free motion embroidery the fabric needs to be taut in the machine embroidery hoop.

- Choose a new needle in the correct size for the fabric. Synthetic fabrics often cause skipped stitches; consult the needle chart in Chapter Three.

- Check the needle to see that it is correctly inserted in the needle holder.

- Check the needle and bobbin threads for correct threading.

- If you are new to free motion embroidery use a darning foot.

- Threads may catch on the needle plate if it is scratched or nicked. Bring the needle plate to your dealer to be smoothed or purchase a new one.

- Interfacing or stabilizer may be necessary to give the fabric body enough to prevent the fabric from puckering or following the needle as it goes up, both recurrent reasons for skipped stitches.

- The bobbin and bobbin case both need to be free of lint and thread fragments.

LOOPS OF THREAD ON THE UNDERSIDE OF THE FABRIC

- Remember that the presser foot engages the top tension when lowered. Leaving it up results in a continuous row of loops.

- Check the needle thread as it may be threaded incorrectly.

- The bobbin thread may be too tight or the needle tension too loose.

BOBBIN THREAD SHOWS ON THE SURFACE

- Needle tension is too tight.

- Bobbin thread is too loose.

- Needle and bobbin thread are of different weights.

NO BOBBIN THREAD SHOWS ON THE REVERSE OF THE EMBROIDERY

- The needle thread is very loose.

- The bobbin thread is much too tight.

NEEDLE BREAKS

- It is common for beginners in free motion embroidery to move the hoop by jerking it while the needle is in motion. This often bends the needle, forcing it to hit the needle plate and break. Practice moving the hoop more smoothly.

- Check the needle to ensure that it is inserted all the way into the needle holder.

- Check to make sure that the needle is not bent or blunt.

- If the top or needle thread tension is too tight a needle may break while stitching.

- Use the correct needle for the thread and fabric being embroidered. See the needle chart in Chapter Three.

- The wrong needle plate may be in place. If you have selected a zigzag pattern and have a straight stitch needle plate in position the needle will crash into the needle plate and break.

- Double and triple needles break most often because they crash into the zigzag needle plate. If your machine has a double needle button use it to limit how wide a zigzag the machine will take. If you do not have this feature use the hand wheel to slowly move through the complete pattern before sewing at top speed.

BOBBIN THREAD BREAKS

- Bobbin tension may be too tight.

- Bobbin may be incorrectly threaded.

- Needle thread may be incorrectly threaded.

- Thread may be wound on the bobbin unevenly or wound over another color and type of thread.

- The bobbin thread may not have been brought up to the surface of the needle plate properly.

- The needle plate may be scratched or nicked. Your dealer can repair or replace the needle plate.

- The needle may be bent or blunt.

- The bobbin case may be incorrectly inserted.

- The bobbin may be inserted the wrong way in the bobbin case.

- There may be lint or thread fragments in the bobbin case or shuttle area.

- Excess thread may be wound on the bobbin.

NO STITCH IS SEWN EVEN THOUGH THE MACHINE IS THREADED

- The needle may be inserted into the needle holder backwards.

- The needle may not be inserted high enough into the needle holder.

- The fabric may not be lying flat on the needle plate at the moment the stitch is taken. Tighten the fabric if it is in a hoop or stabilize the fabric.

- The needle may be threaded in the wrong direction. Check your sewing machine manual.

SEWING MACHINE IS MAKING PECULIAR SOUNDS

- Stop stitching as soon as you hear an odd sound. Continuing will only compound the problem, especially if the thread is jamming in the shuttle.

- The needle or bobbin thread may be incorrectly threaded.

- The hook and race may need oil. Check your manual.

- Presser bar was not engaged while sewing.

- The bobbin area may be clogged with lint or fragments of thread.

FABRIC PUCKERS OR TUNNELS

Fabric tunnels are seen on the surface of the embroidery and are identified by the fabric forming a convex shape, especially under a satin stitch.

- Needle thread or bobbin tension may be too tight.

- Fabric may be too light weight for the density of the stitching and the thickness of the thread. Stabilize the fabric.

- Stitches may be too long or too short, and so you will need to increase or decrease the stitch length or width.

- Fabric may have been jerked away from the machine, causing the fabric to pucker.

- In free motion embroidery it is possible to stitch so densely that the surrounding fabric puckers. Add additional stabilizer or try the new hot water stabilizer called Melt-A-Way or Heat-Away (see Source List).

- The fabric may be too loose in the machine embroidery hoop.

UNEVEN STITCHES

- An incorrect needle is being used for the fabric and thread selected.

- You may be pulling or pushing the fabric while sewing. Allow the feed dogs to move the fabric.

- Needle thread tension is too loose. Tighten slightly and try stitching again on a sample of fabric.

- Check to make sure the sewing machine is properly threaded.

- The needle is incorrectly inserted into the needle holder or is bent or blunt.

- The needle may be worn, of poor quality or poorly polished.

THE FABRIC IS NOT FEEDING SMOOTHLY UNDER THE PRESSER FOOT

- The feed dogs were not raised after free motion embroidery mode was used.

- An improper presser foot is in use. It is imperative that the embroidery or satin stitch foot be used for embroidery other than free motion embroidery.

- The feed dogs may be packed with lint.

- The stitch length may be at zero, which prohibits the feed dogs from moving the fabric.

BOBBIN HAS WOUND UNEVENLY

- The thread has been attached to the bobbin incorrectly.

- The proper thread route for bobbin filling has not been followed.

- The thread has fallen out of the thread guides mid-way during winding.

- The sewing machine motor has been run erratically.

- The thread guide may be bent and thus not allowing the thread to wind evenly.

- The bobbin rewind mechanism may need to be adjusted by your dealer.

Appendix

SHOPPER'S CHECKLIST FOR A SEWING MACHINE

Here is a checklist to take with you when you shop for a sewing machine. Not all of these features and accessories are found on any one machine. You will need to decide which features are most important to you and which you can live without or improvise.

Machine A _____

Machine B _____

Machine C _____

Machine A	Machine B	Machine C	
_____	_____	_____	Do feed dogs lower?
_____	_____	_____	Must feed dogs be covered?
_____	_____	_____	Are presser feet transparent?
_____	_____	_____	Does machine straight stitch only?
_____	_____	_____	Does machine straight stitch and zigzag only?
_____	_____	_____	Does machine have 12 or fewer utility stitches?
_____	_____	_____	How many pre-programmed stitches are there?
_____	_____	_____	What is the widest zigzag width?
_____	_____	_____	Is zigzag adjusted by knob or push button?
_____	_____	_____	Does machine stitch maxi stitches?
_____	_____	_____	Computer interface for custom designs?
_____	_____	_____	Electronic foot pedal?
_____	_____	_____	Power cord retractable?
_____	_____	_____	Needle stop in both up and down positions?
_____	_____	_____	Can the speed of the machine be changed?
_____	_____	_____	Single stitch be taken when foot pedal depressed?
_____	_____	_____	Can a single pattern be stitched?
_____	_____	_____	How many needle positions are there?
_____	_____	_____	Sew with twin and triple needles?
_____	_____	_____	Is there a guarded width for multi-needle sewing?
_____	_____	_____	Is the spool holder vertical?
_____	_____	_____	Is the spool holder horizontal?
_____	_____	_____	How many spool holders are there?
_____	_____	_____	Is it easy to change presser feet?
_____	_____	_____	Is it easy to change needle?
_____	_____	_____	Is it a slant or vertical needle machine?
_____	_____	_____	Is it easy to adjust the thread tension?
_____	_____	_____	Is it easy to adjust the bobbin tension?
_____	_____	_____	Is there a bobbin thread monitor?

SHOPPER'S CHECKLIST FOR A SEWING MACHINE *(continued)*

Machine A   _____

Machine B   _____

Machine C   _____

Machine A	Machine B	Machine C	
_____	_____	_____	Does bobbin fit on spool pin?
_____	_____	_____	Is there a built-in needle threader?
_____	_____	_____	How heavy is the machine?
_____	_____	_____	Is the carry case light and protective?
_____	_____	_____	How large is the sewing table?
_____	_____	_____	Is the sewing table easy to use?
_____	_____	_____	Is there a mirror image function?
_____	_____	_____	Sewing machine feet/accessories?
_____	_____	_____	Satin stitch foot available?
_____	_____	_____	Darning foot available?
_____	_____	_____	Cording/pintucking foot available?
_____	_____	_____	Quilting bar available?
_____	_____	_____	Fringe or marker foot available?
_____	_____	_____	Open toe embroidery foot available?
_____	_____	_____	Can I purchase extra bobbin case?
_____	_____	_____	Lint brush available?
_____	_____	_____	Small screw driver available?

Bibliography

Beck, Thomasina. *The Embroiderer's Flowers.* David & Charles: Devon, England, 1992.

Brown, Gail. *Quick Napkin Creations.* Open Chain Publishing, Inc.: Menlo Park, CA, 1990.

Fanning, Robbie, and Tony Fanning. *The Complete Book of Machine Embroidery.* Chilton Book Co.: Radnor, PA, 1986.

Hardinham, Martin. *The Fabric Catalog.* Pocket Books: New York, 1978.

Holmes, Val. *The Machine Embroiderer's Workbook.* BT Batsford Ltd.: London, 1991.

Hurley, Sharon. *Monogramming.* Sharon By The Sea Publishing: Santa Barbara, CA, 1988.

Messent, Jan. *Embroidery and Animals.* BT Batsford Ltd.: London, 1984.

Messent, Jan. *The Embroiderer's Workbook.* St. Martin's Press: New York, 1988.

Natoli, Eugena. *Cats of the World.* Crescent Books: New York, 1987.

Roberts, Sharee Dawn. *Creative Machine Art.* American Quilter's Society, Paducah, KY, 1992.

Russell, Pat. *Lettering for Embroidery.* BT Batsford Ltd.: London, 1971.

Seagroatt, Margaret. *A Basic Textile Book.* Van Nostrand Reinhold Co.: New York, 1975.

Singer. *Decorative Machine Stitching.* Cy DeCosse Inc.: Minnetonka, MN, 1990.

Snook, Barbara. *The Craft of Florentine Embroidery.* Charles Scribner's Sons: New York, 1971.

Sparling, Glenda D. *Wrapped in Fabriqué.* Ranita Corporation, Eugene, OR, 1994.

Springall, Diana. *Design for Embroidery: A Fine Art Approach.* Pelham Books: Middlesex, England, 1988.

Wedd, Dunkin J. A. *Pattern & Texture.* The Studio Publications: New York, 1956.

Williams, Elsa S. *Bargello Florentine Canvas Work.* Van Nostrand Reinhold Co.: New York, 1967.

Williams, Elsa S. *Heritage Embroidery.* Van Nostrand Reinhold Co.: New York, 1967.

Williams, Janice. *Lettering in Embroidery.* BT Batsford Ltd.: London, 1982.

Source List

AARDVARK ADVENTURES
P. O. Box 2449
Livermore, CA 94551-2449
415-443-2687
Shisha mirrors and stabilizers

**AMERICAN CREWEL
AND CANVAS STUDIO**
Rt. 2, Box 224B
Parsonsburg, MD 21849
310-749-0394
Thread and notions

BABY LOCK U. S. A.
P. O. Box 730
St. Louis, MO 63026
314-349-3000
Esante sewing machines and sergers

BERNINA OF AMERICA, INC.
3500 Thayer Court
Aurora, IL 60504-6182
708-978-2500
Sewing machines and sergers

**BROTHER INTERNATIONAL
CORPORATION**
200 Cottontail Lane
Somerset, NJ 08875-6714
201-981-0300
Sewing machines and sergers

CLOTILDE, INC.
2 Sew Smart Way
B8031
Stevens Point, WI 54481-8031
800-772-2891
*Clo-Chalk, Perfect Pleater, Clover Chaco-
line, Horizontal Spool Holder, multiple
cording guide*

DECART, INC.
Lamoille Industrial Park
Box 309
Morrisville, VT 05661
802-888-4217
Fabric paint

DECO ART
P. O. Box 327
Stanford, KY 40484
606-365-3193
Fabric paint

DELTA
2550 Pellissier Place
Whittier, CA 90601
800-423-4135
Fabric paint

ELNA INC.
7642 Washington Avenue South
Eden Prairie, MN 55344
612-941-5519
Sewing machines and sergers

GHEE'S
2620 Centenary Boulevard #3-205
Shreveport, LA 71104
318-226-1701
*Pocketbook frames, fabrics, sewing
notions, and books*

**HEATnBOND
THERM O WEB**
770 Glenn Avenue
Wheeling, IL 60090
708-520-5200
Stabilizers

INKADINKADO INC.
60 Cummings Park
Woburn, MA 01801
617-338-2600
Cards with mat openings

JUKI AMERICA
3555 Lomita Boulevard
Torrance, CA 92680
310-325-5811
Sewing machines and sergers

KEEPSAKE QUILTING
Dover Street
P. O. Box 1459
Meredith, NH 03253
603-279-3351
Batting, sewing, and quilting supplies

MUNDIAL
50 Kerry Place
Norwood, MA 02062
617-762-8310
4" hand clippers and dress-making scissors

NANCY'S NOTIONS LTD.
P. O. Box 683
Beaver Dam, WI 53916-0683
800-833-0690
Complete line of sewing supplies

NEW HOME SEWING MACHINE CO.
100 Hollister Road
Teterboro, NJ 07608
201-440-8080
*Memory Craft 9000 Sewing Machine, silk
and acrylic machine embroidery thread*

PALMER/PLETSCH
P. O. Box 12046
Portland, OR 97212-0046
800-728-3784
Books and sewing supplies

PASSAP-USA
271 West 2950 South
Salt Lake City, UT 84115
801-485-2771
Topjet Vario Steam Iron

PFAFF AMERICAN SALES CORP.
610 Winters Avenue
Paramus, NJ 07653-0566
201-262-7211
7550 Sewing Machine

SCHMETZ NEEDLE CORPORATION
P. O. Box 23438
Knoxville, TN 37933
Sewing machine needles

SCS U. S. A.
Sewing and Craft Supply
9631 N. E. Colfax
Portland, OR 97230
800-547-8025
*Madeira machine embroidery thread and
sewing notions*

SEW ART INTERNATIONAL
P. O. Box 2725
Spring Valley, CA 91978
800-231-2787
*Fringe frames (sets of three) and machine
embroidery thread*

SHARON BY THE SEA
5018 Calle Real
Santa Barbara, CA 93111-1810
805-967-8359
Books

SINGER SEWING CO.
135 Raritan Center Parkway
Edison, NJ 08837-3642
908-225-8844
Quantum XL-100 Sewing Machine

SOURCE MARKETING
600 East 9th
Michigan City, IN 46360
219-873-1000
*Hot water-soluble stabilizer and couching
threads*

SUSAN ROCK
113 Woodhill Road
Bow, NH 03304
603-774-6472 (telephone)
603-774-3223 (fax)
*Machine embroidery thread, Stable Ease
Stabilizer, patterns, and lesson plans for
classes*

TREADLE ART
25834 Nabonne Avenue
Lomita, CA 90717
310-534-5122
*Catalog of sewing supplies; machine
embroidery thread and hoops*

VIKING HUSQVARNA
11760 Berea Road
Cleveland, OH 44111-1601
216-252-3300
Viking #1+ Sewing Machine

WAVERLY
79 Madison Avenue
New York, NY 10016
Fabrics

WEB OF THREAD
3240 Lone Oak Road
Suite 124
Paducah, KY 42003
502-554-8185
*Machine embroidery thread; Perfect Pleat;
and hoops*

Index